Sources of Holocaust Research

Sources of
Holocaust Research

AN ANALYSIS

Raul Hilberg

Ivan R. Dee Chicago

Library of Congress Cataloging-in-Publication Data:
Hilberg, Raul, 1926–
    Sources of Holocaust research : an analysis / Raul Hilberg.
        p. cm.
    Includes bibliographical references (p.) and index.
    ISBN 1-56663-379-6 (alk. paper)
    1. Holocaust, Jewish (1939–1945)—Historiography.   I. Title.

    D804.348 .H56 2001
    940.53'18'072—dc21   2001017217

ERRATA

SOURCES OF HOLOCAUST RESEARCH

On page

23, footnote 21 in its entirety should read:
Directive of Hitler, November 16, 1938, RGB1 I, 1611.

25, the last paragraph should begin with: Any ministry or occupational authority

25, footnote 28 should end with: (Ludwigshafen, 1988), p. 86.

27, the omitted footnote 32 is:
Decree of October 5, 1938, RGB1 I, 1342. A facsimile of a passport is in Schwab, *Echoes*, p. 149.

39, in the top paragraph, period meetings should be: periodic meetings

65, in the top paragraph, the 70th Infantry Division should be: the 707th

82, the middle of footnote 8 should be:
"Reichsbahnoberrat" (the correct designation was Oberreichsbahnrat) Reichardt

91, in footnote 23, RBM1 should be: RMB1

120, in footnote 101, I should be: II

157, in footnote 58, David should be: Dawid

162, in footnote 63, *ocupacji* should be: *okupacji*

185, point 3 should end with: configuration
A new line should begin with: As maxims

196, in the middle paragraph, Photostats should be: photostats

Foreign words and names incorrectly parted, and missing foreign diacritical marks, are not noted in these errata.

Contents

Preface

The annihilation of the Jews on the European continent during World War II was historically a novum which prompted a growing army of researchers to investigate its nature in all of its facets. I have been one of these people, spending many hours in libraries and archives, or occasionally at sites where drastic actions took place. Yet I came to analyze the sources I was using at a late stage of my life. For fifty years I preoccupied myself mainly with the event itself, thinking of sources as raw material that would enable me to fashion a description of the destruction process. I could not write about this complex phenomenon without searching for evidence in pieces of paper, sifting them, combining them, immersing myself in the atmosphere of the time when they had been composed, measuring the pulse of the whole development and assessing its gravity.

But then I stopped to ask myself: what is the nature of my sources? They are not identical to the subject matter. They have their own history and qualities, which are different from the actions they depict and which require a separate approach. I persuaded myself to undertake the probe, imagining it to be relatively simple and not all that demanding. After all, I had lived with these materials and they had become familiar to me. To the degree that I had initial doubts about such a project, they were centered on its worthwhileness. The questions seemed too easy, the answers too obvious, the insights too small, but it did not take long before the true dimensions of the problem began to emerge.

I detected pitfalls in my first outlines. Again and again I had to stop myself lest I fall into a trap. Dictionaries beside me, I pondered the choice of words for headings. Had I covered everything? Was there an overlap? A tautology? A contradiction? Sometimes it was difficult to select an appropriate example. Almost every source illustrates not one point but several. Here was yet another beginning for me. An item I had studied would suddenly seem strange, or a document from which I had written down only the "essence" in the age before photocopiers would now be incomplete. The most banal features of a source now acquired importance, and the mass of material, as if under an x-ray machine, took on an entirely different appearance. At the halfway mark of my labor I recognized that what I had considered an afterthought turned out to be a challenge instead.

This book is my attempt to describe the sources as such. It is not a manual or epistemological treatise but an analysis divided into five chapters that deal in succession with the types of materials, their composition, style, content, and usability.

The first step is an exterior examination of the sources. They are introduced and classified by type, with explanations. Sometimes the differences are readily apparent. A spoon once used by a camp inmate is a source, and so is a letter on official stationery, or the testimony of a survivor on tape. These items are visibly not the same. Often, however, one must make finer distinctions. When, for example, a half-million pages are encountered in a single collection, the criterion for determining which document belongs to what category is a question of who addressed whom in the correspondence. All these varieties are covered in the opening chapter.

The next requisite is an interior view. If one thinks about the critical commentary devoted to literary or artistic works, replete with dissections of their structure, style, and ideas, one cannot help noticing that this bountiful attention is not lavished on historical sources, which are commonly deemed lifeless. Yet each source has a definite configuration, a characteristic style, and a highly selective content. These topics take up the following three chapters.

Finally, one should ask what can be extracted from the sources. That is a twofold proposition, one a matter of the intrinsic problems presented by the material itself, the other a set of external conditions. The usability of the sources is discussed in the concluding chapter.

A penultimate draft of the manuscript was read by my son David Hilberg and my old friend Eric Marder. Both made suggestions that brought more clarity to obscure passages and more smoothness to abrupt transitions. My association with Eric began many years ago when we walked home from high school together. It continued over the decades whenever we met, talking about the purposes of our work and the meaning of our lives. I freely solicited his advice and comments, and he was always ready to help when I found myself in a quandary. Such intellectual support is very rare, and I have relied on it for sixty years.

RAUL HILBERG

Burlington, Vermont
May 2001

Sources of Holocaust Research

ONE

Types of Sources

◻ The sources of information about the Holocaust may be separated into distinct types of material. This systematization should be clear-cut. In the simplest way, structures and objects that in a conventional sense are regarded as three-dimensional may be placed in one category, and flat items in another. Each of these groups may then be divided further, so that all the principal subcategories are identified, explained, and illustrated.

Structures are fixed on specific sites, whereas objects are smaller and movable. Not much is left of whole compounds, like ghettos and camps, or of mass graves. Most of them are gone. The buildings of the largest ghetto, in Warsaw, were razed by the Germans after the deportations of 1943. Today a newly built cluster of houses along redirected streets occupies the space. The constellation of three annihilation camps in Bełżec, Sobibór, and Treblinka was similarly leveled before the arrival of the Red Army. The bodies in most of the mass graves of eastern Europe were systematically removed and burned by a special SS-Kommando. Several sites that had not been obliterated by the perpetrators were immediately or gradually transformed by the victorious Allies. The wooden barracks of the Birkenau section of Auschwitz had to be burned down by a Soviet sanitation unit to prevent epidemics. The ravines at Babi Yar in Kiev, where a major massacre took place, are no more.

Still standing are small apartment houses in which the Viennese Jews were concentrated for deportation. Virtually pristine is the Lublin camp, also known as Maydanek, which was hastily abandoned by retreating German forces. The brick buildings in the main camp of Auschwitz survived, and in nearby Birkenau the ruins of the gas chambers blown up by the Germans at the last moment were left in place. In the village of Serniki, Ukraine, an Australian team dug up a grave containing hundreds of bodies that a German cremation Kommando had not destroyed.[1] Limited archeological explorations at Bełżec took place shortly after the war and again in the 1990s to determine the configuration of the former camp. But that is nearly all. The many facts of the Holocaust cannot be recovered from such physical remains.

The situation is not very different with regard to objects of various kinds. Railroad boxcars of the type that carried Jewish deportees stand on a track near Treblinka, and one can be found in the United States Holocaust Memorial Museum in Washington, D.C. Also preserved are planks with which prefabricated barracks (horse stables—*Pferdestallbaracken*) were assembled in Auschwitz for inmates. Bales of cloth with the yellow star have been shown in the Jewish Museum in Vienna, and individual stars worn by Jews may be viewed in various public exhibits. Paper money and coins that were currency in

1. A film of the exhumation, made by the Australian Special Investigations Unit, was brought by me to the United States Holocaust Memorial Museum.

the Łódź ghetto, and notes that were circulated in the ghetto of Theresienstadt, are still common. In Auschwitz, some of the luggage that Jews had brought along is kept under glass, and so are eyeglasses and women's long hair. Shoes gathered by the SS in the Bełżec-Sobibór-Treblinka complex fill entire barracks in the Lublin camp. A Gypsy cart, a fishing boat that carried Jews to safety from Denmark to Sweden, the rusted weapon of a resister—these are the other kinds of objects that still exist, but there is little else.

Sources that are physically flat may be divided into two media: pictorial and verbal. Visual materials comprise blueprints, sketches, drawings, photographs, and contemporary films. Once again, one is faced with comparative scarcity. Only photographs make up recognizable quantities in this group, and even here the collection becomes small if one subtracts the scenes of pre-Nazi times—the "world that was"—and concentrates on photography inside the Nazi power sphere. The depictions of the earlier period help define a baseline, showing how people lived, what sorts of possessions they had, and what kinds of schools, workplaces, or resorts they went to before destructive measures descended upon them. Later pictorial sources include "action" films and photographs, sweeping a ghetto from the entrances guarded by police to bodies on the sidewalk inside, or showing a group of Jews boarding a deportation train.

The information in photographs is different from verbal descriptions. The details are not the same. Although a snapshot is momentary, it would not be easy to summarize all that it contains in words. Often a witness would simply not think of including features that the operator of a camera would capture automatically. This is true of all photographs, regardless of whether a scene was staged or candid. Each of them is revealing and each tells a story. One might look at a posed group portrait of Dutch Jews at a wedding, wearing their best clothes with the obligatory Jewish star;[2] or Jews in the Łódź ghetto, sitting in a semicircle in coats and caps on the pavement with their backs to one another, apparently slurping soup from their pails;[3] or the gentile Parisian intellectual Jean-Paul Sartre, pipe in his mouth, having a glass of wine in the Café de Flore in 1943.[4] Jews are the most frequent figures in Holocaust photographs, but they contributed the smallest portion of the photographic record. Eventually their cameras were confiscated,[5] and the relatively few photographers in the Jewish community worked clandestinely to record the fate of Jewry on film. By contrast, many German photographs reflect a propagandistic aim. Some Jews were selected for a picture because they were unkempt, or a regimented production line might have been set up on a clean floor so that one could see Jewish laborers made "useful" under strict German discipline. Finally, there are chance photographs—most of them by spectators but some by members of professional German propaganda companies—which were forbidden and which are sought out for that very reason. But a researcher may not be able to determine the place, time, or other particulars of what is shown.

Verbal sources constitute the great bulk of the material at hand. By the beginning of the Nazi regime, Europe was

2. The photograph portrays the wedding of Samuel Schryver in Amsterdam, 1942. United States Holocaust Memorial Museum Photo Archives, Desig. #506.565, W/S #08726, CD #0031. Husband and wife were killed in Sobibór on July 9, 1943.

3. Mendel Grossman, *With a Camera in the Ghetto* (New York, 1977), pp. 12–13.

4. Gilles Perrault and Pierre Azema, *Paris Under the Occupation* (New York, 1989), p. 115.

5. See Ministrialdirigent Groth (Finance Ministry) to Oberfinanzpräsidenten (not including Prague), August 31, 1942, referring to an earlier Security Police directive, Nuremberg trials document NG-5312.

Dutch Jews at a wedding in 1942, wearing their best clothes with the obligatory Jewish star.

highly literate and produced an enormous quantity of written words. The word flow was generated in public and private domains by ranking officials and by ordinary clerks, by trained specialists and by individuals whose education had stopped at age fourteen or thereabouts. Generally the texts are typed, but one can also find handwritten pages ranging from short field reports of low-level military or police offices to lengthy private diaries. Inasmuch as measures against Jews covered areas under German control as well as states allied with Germany, the languages of this output number more than twenty. German is paramount, but satellite governments added a substantial volume of enactments. Even in occupied regions, indigenous offices and formations like municipalities and police battalions dealt with internal matters in their own languages. Similarly, Jewish councils and community organizations usually employed the national language of the country in daily communications between their departments and branches: Romanian in Romania, French in France, Dutch in the Netherlands. Within the prewar boundaries of Poland, the extent of Jewish assimilation influenced the choice of language for the internal records of the councils: Polish in Warsaw and Lublin, Yiddish in Bialystok and Vilna.

Linguistic diversity could appear in a single place. The files of native administrations in German-occupied territories were bifurcated: the local language, plus German for all correspondence with the German overlords. The same situation applied also to Jewish councils. German was prescribed, whether in Warsaw or Pinsk, for reports or petitions to German supervisors. Inside one or another Jewish bureaucracy, more than one language could be used for exchanges among Jewish council members and functionaries. The Łódź ghetto chronicle, which was composed by Jewish journalists or writers over a period of four years as an internal record of daily events, and which totaled about a million words, was begun in

Polish and continued in German.[6] The protocols of meetings in the Jewish council of the Kaunas ghetto shifted from Lithuanian to German and then to Yiddish.[7] In the division of "special tasks" of the Jewish council in Slovakia, the reports of preparations in transit camps for deportation were made in Slovak or German, depending on the writer.[8]

The authors of private diaries wrote in German, French, Dutch, Polish, Yiddish, and other languages. Comparatively few are in Hebrew. In postwar testimony, former perpetrators and local bystanders availed themselves of their native tongues. Jewish survivors returning to their homelands continued to use the language of their youth.[9] Those from eastern Europe who settled in different regions of the world wrote a number of memoirs during the first postwar years in Yiddish.[10]

6. Lucjan Dobrosycki, ed., *The Chronicle of the Łódź Ghetto 1941–1944* (New Haven, 1984), pp. ix–xvi. The English-language edition consists of excerpts.

7. Lithuanian Central Archives, Fond 973, Opis 3, Folder 4.

8. Yad Vashem collection M-5 (18) and M-5 (21).

9. Mostly in Polish in Poland. See Daniel Grinberg, "Unpublished Diaries and Memoirs in the State Archives of the Jewish Historical Institute in Poland," in Robert Moses Shapiro, ed., *Holocaust Chronicles* (New York, 1999), pp. 257–264. In French, the diary of the French Jewish leader Raymond-Raoul Lambert, *Carnet d'un témoin* (Paris, 1985). A diary in Romanian that was published in German translation is Miriam Korber, *Deportiert* (Konstanz, 1993). In Italian, a memoir by Primo Levi, *Se questo e un uomo* (Turin, 1958). In Dutch, a memoir by G. L. Durlacher, *Streepen aan de hemel* (Amsterdam, 1985). A memoir in Greek, published in English translation in Athens after its author died there, is Errikos Sevillias, *Athens-Auschwitz* (Athens, 1983).

10. For example, Bernard Goldstein, *Finf Yor im Warshaver Ghetto* (New York, 1947). The book, by a leader of the Socialist Jewish Bund in Poland, appeared also in English and German translation. Several Yiddish memoirs were first published in the original in Buenos Aires. The diary of Abraham Lewin (Warsaw ghetto) was written in Yiddish before the deportations started, and in Hebrew thereafter. See his *A Cup of Tears* (Oxford, England, 1988), with a note by the editor, Antony Polonsky, p. 55. There are also translations of translations, not always clearly identified as such in the published books.

Later they composed accounts, sometimes with professional help, in the languages of their new countries, including English but also German.[11]

For purposes of analysis, the verbal sources may be further divided into two groups, one containing all the items produced before the collapse of Nazi Germany, the other comprising the materials created retrospectively after the war. To hold this distinction in place, the contemporaneous materials will be called "documents," and the recollections "testimony."

Like all artifacts, the documentary collections were subject to attrition until a finite quantity remained. Quite a few German records went up in flames when the buildings in which they were stored were hit by bombs in air raids.[12] Similarly, Jewish ghetto correspondence as well as private diaries in Warsaw were lost during the revolt of 1943, and a year later in the larger Polish uprising.[13] German documents having only transitory value were not necessarily preserved beyond the period of their usefulness.[14] Moreover, upon the approach of Al-

11. Rudolf Vrba and Alan Bestic, *I Cannot Forgive* (New York, 1964). Vrba is the survivor. Filip Müller (with literary collaboration by Helmut Freitag), *Sonderbehandlung* (Munich, 1997). Müller, like Vrba, is an Auschwitz survivor. For yet another variant, see Yirmeyahu Oskar Neumann, a former chairman of the Jewish council in Slovakia, whose German-language memoir appeared untranslated in Israel under the title *Im Schatten des Todes* (Tel Aviv, 1956).

12. For example, the "Central Office for Jewish Emigration" (Gestapo) in Vienna. Directorate of the Police to Landesgericht (court) in Vienna, January 13, 1962, Dokumentationsarchiv des österreichischen Widerstandes, document 19061/2.

13. Joseph Kermish, ed., *To Live with Honor and Die with Honor* (Jerusalem, 1986), introduction, pp. xv–xvi. The Hebrew-language diary by the commander of a large segment of the resisters in the Warsaw ghetto, Mordechai Anielewicz, was lost at that time along with almost all internal records of the council.

14. See the instructions pertaining to deportation trains by the Generaldirektion der Ostbahn/30H (signed by Theodor Schmid) to railway stations from Częstochowa to Warsaw, March 26, 1943, stating: "Save until

lied forces, many office files were routinely destroyed. In railway stations it was common practice to dispose of all items, not only those under lock and key, in the course of retreats.[15] Regional authorities did the same. Four days after Kraków was abandoned by the German army, Generalgouverneur Hans Frank, who had ruled a large part of Poland from that city, and three of his assistants burned most of the folders they had brought along to German soil.[16] By February 20, 1945, Propaganda Minister Joseph Goebbels ordered the systematic destruction of Germany's secret and sensitive materials, including those dealing with Jews.[17] Taken as a whole, the considerable size of the missing aggregate is revealed in the gaping holes of what remains.

Nevertheless the accumulation of paper was so large that if the collection of an office was not incinerated in its entirety, single pages with even the most drastic content could not be torn out at the last moment. An example from Romania is a case in point. The story begins in October 1941 when an explosion ripped through the headquarters of the 10th Romanian Division in the newly captured city of Odessa, killing the commander and members of his staff. Marshal Ion Antonescu, the Romanian dictator, told his staff officer to send out a telegraphic order that a building crammed with Odessa

May 6, 1943." Zentrale Stelle der Landesjustizverwaltungen in Ludwigsburg, Collection Polen, Film 6.

15. Eugen Kreidler, *Die Eisenbahnen im Machtbereich der Achsenmächte während des Zweiten Weltkrieges* (Göttingen, 1975), p. 9.

16. Diary of Generalgouverneur Frank, January 21, 1945, U.S. National Archives Record Group 238, T 992, Roll 12. A few portions of the diary itself were lost after the war in the course of preparations for the first Nuremberg trial. Stanislaw Piotrowski, *Hans Frank's Diary* (Warsaw, 1961), p. 11.

17. Order by Goebbels, February 20, 1945. The original document was once located in the Federal Records Center, Alexandria, Va., Footlocker 46/19. At the end of the war, Goebbels was also the Plenipotentiary for the Total War Effort.

Jews be blown up in retaliation. "This order," said the text, "is to be destroyed after reading," but the handwritten draft in Bucharest was found more than fifty years later in its proper dossier.[18] Sometimes it was a field office that neglected to destroy correspondence emanating from a central agency. The many copies and the many collections, the rapid retreats at the end of the war—all this contributed to the survival of records that the Allies seized, occasionally in remote storage facilities. What was left fills hundreds of archives today.

The surviving documents consist of those that were open from the day they were produced and those that were closed to outsiders until the end. The published portion includes laws, regulations, and judicial decisions; all documents issued to persons; directories, census data, and the like; and pamphlets, newspaper reports, recorded broadcasts, and so forth.

Anti-Jewish laws and regulations alone numbered in the thousands. This proliferation stemmed from a need, inchoate in the Nazi "movement," not to stand still. There were three hiatus years—1934, 1936, and 1937—marked by little activity, but they were bridged by a growing pressure to go on, to separate Jewry from Germany wholly, to impose progressively severe restrictions on Jews, and to widen the range of prohibitions until they infused every sphere of life. Any subject could be on the table. Jewish physicians were not allowed to have

18. The document, dated October 24, 1941, is in the United States Holocaust Memorial Museum Archives, Record Group 23.003 (Romanian National Archives), Roll 12, Fond Fourth Army, Dosar 870. See also the additional correspondence in 870. A translation by Radu Ioanid, who discovered this item and generously shared his knowledge and insights with me, is in his *The Holocaust in Romania* (Chicago, 2000), p. 179. In nearby Dalnik, a warehouse holding Jews who had been machine-gunned was blown up on October 25, 1941. Indictment of Generals Nicolae Macici and Constantin Trestioreanu, May 3, 1945, in Jean Ancel, ed., *Documents Concerning the Fate of Romanian Jewry During the Holocaust* (New York, [1986]), VI, 60–61.

German patients.[19] Jewish entrepreneurs were deprived of their industrial enterprises.[20] Jews were prohibited from wearing a uniform[21] or sending out carrier pigeons.[22] Due to the fact that Germany, unlike France, Slovakia, Romania, and Bulgaria, had no central agency that planned anti-Jewish decrees, these measures were issued by a variety of authorities, both central and local. From the "Old Reich" (*Altreich*, with the 1937 borders), the anti-Jewish regime was extended to annexed and occupied territories. In addition, the German model served as inspiration to other countries in Germany's orbit for their own anti-Jewish laws. Several states that were possible havens for Jews would set up legal and administrative barriers to admission, or they would limit the duration of the asylum or restrict the freedom of the refugees and escapees.

The several types of German enactments are ranged in the following hierarchy:

Law (*Gesetz*)
Decree (*Verordnung*)
Implementation Decree (*Durchführungsverordnung*)
Directive (*Anordnung*)
Specification for Implementation (*Durchführungsbestimmung*)
Announcement (*Bekanntmachung*)

All of these measures were considered public lawmaking acts (*Rechtsetzungsakte*).[23]

---

19. Decree of July 25, 1938, *Reichsgesetzblatt* (abbr. RGBl) I, 949.
20. Decree of December 3, 1938, RGBl I, 1709
21. Directive of Hitler, November 29, 1938, RGBl I, 1611.22. Decree of November 29, 1938, RGBl I, 1749.
22. Decree of November 29, 1938, RGBl I, 1749.
23. See Generalkommissar in Riga/II (signed Sommerlatte) to Gebietskommissare and others, December 7, 1942, National Archives, Record

The law, as the highest enactment, might be signed by Hitler himself and by the ministers responsible for its creation. The first minister's signature represented the ministry primarily in charge of the drafting. Decrees, usually signed by a minister, could stand alone, or they could be numbered to signify that they contained provisions for carrying out a particular law named in their title. The Reich Citizenship Law of 1935 provided that only persons of German or related blood could be citizens. Subsequently thirteen decrees were published in pursuance of that law. Twelve of the thirteen dealt with Jews, one with Poles.[24]

Whether something was a law or a decree was mostly a reflection of the rank of the signer rather than the intrinsic importance of the subject. A regulation, worked out by the Justice Ministry, breaking the obligation of contract for German landlords who wished to evict Jewish tenants, was a law because it was signed by Hitler as well as other high-ranking officials.[25] A later measure providing for the marking of the Jews with a star was a police decree (*Polizeiverordnung*), signed only by Reinhard Heydrich, the chief of the Reich Main Security Office, whose rank was below that of a minister.[26] A directive (*Anordnung*) could suffice for the confiscation of foreign currency, bank accounts, gold, silver, and other items belonging to Jews in the city of Vilnius (Vilna). It was signed by the

Group 242, T 459, Roll 22. For a similar categorization of French enactments into *loi, décret, arrêté, circulaire*, and *communiqué*, see Centre de Documentation Juive Contemporaine, *Les juifs sous l'occupation* (Paris, 1982). The book contains texts of French and German regulations in France.

24. Text of the Reich Citizenship Law of 1935 in RGBl I, 1146. All thirteen of the implementation decrees from 1935 to 1943 were published in the *Reichsgesetzblatt*. For an analysis, see Uwe Adam, *Judenpolitik im Dritten Reich* (Tübingen, 1972), pp. 245–246.

25. Tenancy Law of April 30, 1939, RGBl I, 864. The landlord had only to show that the Jewish tenant had access to other accommodations.

26. Decree of September 1, 1941, RGBl I, 547.

local *Gebietskommissar.*[27] An announcement (*Bekanntmachung*) in Germany was used to compel Jews to show their identification cards unasked.[28]

Laws and decrees were published in the principal legal gazette, the *Reichsgesetzblatt*. A variety of regulations appeared in the official publications of ministries, notably the *Reichsministerialblatt* of the Interior Ministry, the *Reichsarbeitsblatt* of the Labor Ministry, the *Reichssteuerblatt* for tax measures, or the *Reichsärzteblatt* for the practice of medicine. In the Netherlands, Bohemia-Moravia, and other occupied territories under civilian rule, each potentate had his own *Verordnungsblatt*, and a subregional jurisdiction like the *Generalkommissariat* Byelorussia or Latvia would have an *Amtsblatt*. Other countries had their gazettes, for example the French *Journal officiel de l'état français* or the Romanian *Monitorul Oficial*.

Any ministry of occupational authority could take action when an appropriate stage called for new anti-Jewish measures, such as reductions of wages or of food rations, but prior consultation was necessary if the contemplated step touched an area traditionally administered by another agency. In December 1938, Heinrich Himmler, who was in charge of a collective body styled "SS and Police," availed himself of his access to newspapers for the publication of a provisional police ordinance invalidating drivers' licenses held by Jews. Normally the regulation of all forms of transportation was in the hands of the Transport Ministry. In this case Himmler not

27. Directive signed by Hans Hingst, September 3, 1941, *Amtsblatt des Generalkommissars in Kauen* (Kaunas, or Kovno), November 22, 1942, p. 26.

28. Announcement of July 28, 1938, RGBl I, 922. A Bekanntmachung could also be local. See facsimile of a draft by the mayor of Ludwigshafen, May 16, 1939, about the registration of Jewish-owned houses renting to non-Jews and non-Jewish-owned houses renting to Jews in Hermann M. Morweiser, *Pfälzer Juden und IG Farben* (Ludwigshafen, 1988), p. 8629. Adam, *Judenpolitik*, pp. 213, 244.

only invaded the domain of this ministry but did so in a novel manner, omitting the established requirement of placing such a text in the *Ministerialblatt* of the Interior Ministry. When the complaint of a Jew reached the highest court in Germany, the *Reichsgericht*, it ruled that inasmuch as the foray had not been contested by any of the "Highest Reich Authorities," as ministries and equivalent agencies were known, it had the force of law.[29]

On November 23, 1938, a new Jewish newspaper, titled *Jüdisches Nachrichtenblatt*, which took the place of previously existing Jewish papers, was inaugurated on a biweekly basis in Berlin. A second *Nachrichtenblatt* was published in Vienna, followed by the *Zydowske Listy* in Prague, the *Gazeta Zydowska* in Kraków, and the *Gazeta Evreiasca* in Bucharest. These papers became a conduit through which governmental regulations came to the notice of the Jewish population. Some measures were transmitted to the Jewish communities in writing, but later in Germany, when the Gestapo as a component of the Security Police arrogated to itself an increasing say in Jewish matters, many oral instructions received from the Gestapo were printed in the *Nachrichtenblatt* of Berlin. By November 1941 the profusion of regulations scattered in various gazettes and in the *Nachrichtenblatt* prompted the Gestapo, which no longer had an overview, to ask the Jewish community for a listing, by subject matter, of all the regulations that had been issued.[30]

A control system consisting of identity cards, papers, and the like was instituted by a variety of agencies in most regions of German-dominated Europe. As of 1938, all Jewish adults of German nationality were required to carry an identification

29. Adam, *Judenpolitik*, pp. 213, 244.
30. See the reports in the Leo Baeck Institute, Microfilm 66. The Berlin edition of the *Nachrichtenblatt* continued publication through 1942; the Viennese appeared for a somewhat longer time.

card (*Kennkarte*) marked with a "J."[31] Also that year, the German passports of Jews were marked with a large red "J,"[32] and in 1940 the "J" was affixed to ration cards.[33] This kind of marking was already anticipated by the University of Freiburg in 1933, when it required non-Aryan students to carry yellow instead of the regular brown identification cards.[34] Afterward all sorts of personal documents appeared. The internment camp of Westerbork in the Netherlands issued a labor card.[35] Hungarian Jews in forced labor companies had their own special registration certificates and paybooks, the latter marked "Jew" (*Zsidó*),[36] and in Romania Jews could obtain cards for exemption from forced labor, the *carnete de scutire*.[37] The extent of the regimentation is illustrated in the following list of items collected from a single ghetto, Theresienstadt, which housed aged deportees from Germany and most of the Jews of Bohemia and Moravia:

Night passes
Certificates bearing an identification number

31. Decree of July 23, 1938, RGBl I, 922. A facsimile of a Kennkarte is in Jüdisches Historisches Institut Warschau, *Faschismus—Getto—Massenmord* (Berlin [East], 1961), pp. 260–261. For a French identification card marked with a "J" and dated as early as July 17, 1940, see Henry Schwab, *The Echoes That Remain* (Weston, Mass., 1992), p. 147. For a Norwegian card, see the facsimile in Oskar Mendelsohn, *Jødenes Historie i Norge* (Oslo, 1986), II, 51.

33. Food and Agriculture Ministry (signed by Georg Narten) to Food Offices, March 11, 1940, Nuremberg trials document NI-14581.

34. Albrecht Götz von Olenhusen, "Die 'nichtarischen' Studenten an den deutschen Hochschulen," *Vierteljahrshefte für Zeitgeschichte* 14 (1986): 185.

35. Facsimile in Schwab, *Echoes*, p. 98.

36. See a facsimile of a registration certificate and a paybook (the latter marked *Zsidó* [Jew]) in Randolph Braham, *The Politics of Genocide* (New York, 1981), I, 303, 324, 326. The registration is that of Braham himself.

37. See the correspondence about these cards in Ancel, *Documents*, VII, *passim*. The volume has no cards in facsimiles.

Certificates certifying that the bearer was "prominent"
Notices of former German or Austro-Hungarian officers
Passes to attend a funeral
Recommendations to allow bearers to have a bath
Orders to vacate houses temporarily for fumigation
Death certificates
Ration cards
Ration cards for heavy laborers
Milk ration cards
Theresienstadt bank books
Permits to buy clothes
Permits to buy specific clothes for specified amounts
Permits to exchange articles of clothing
Labor certificates
Hospital admissions
Permits to visit the coffee house
Blue cards for Jewish ghetto guards[38]

Most of the cards and certificates in Theresienstadt were produced by the "Jewish Self-Administration" in the ghetto. These documents and those of other places disappeared rapidly, either when they became obsolete or when their possessors died before the end of the war. What remains, aside from passports and Kennkarten, which are still numerous, is a relative handful of specimens, and these are not necessarily all the different documents that existed at the time. Even rarer are the forgeries by means of which some Jews survived.

Among the printed documents were also reference books and periodicals containing statistics and lists of names. Quite a

---

38. H. G. Adler, ed., *Die verheimlichte Wahrheit* (Tübingen, 1958), *passim*. All items, except the blue card, are reproduced in this book in facsimile. Most of the Theresienstadt inmates were deported for gassing or shooting. Most of the others died in the ghetto.

few census data were published in the volumes and issues of *Statistik des Deutschen Reiches* and *Wirtschaft und Statistik*. They are preserved in large libraries. More specialized information in tabular form is contained in various books. Most widespread among publications with names were telephone directories. Not many years after the war, however, the thin directory of 1938 for Warsaw was as scarce as the annual German compilation of business leaders and officials concerned with the economy, *Wer leitet*. Also not plentiful are copies of German newspapers, particularly those published in occupied territories, notably the *Krakauer Zeitung* in Kraków, the *Donauzeitung* in Belgrade, and the *Deutsche Ukraine-Zeitung* in Lutsk, which frequently featured summaries of laws and statistics, and events such as ghetto formation.

From time to time the underground, Jewish and non-Jewish, produced papers, leaflets, and placards, which followed the political lines of their originators: Communist, nationalist, Zionist, and so forth. Some of these items were political wake-up calls, with admonitions or warnings. Added to these messages were Allied ones, for example a lengthy British pamphlet in the German language titled "The Other Side" (*Die andere Seite*). Noteworthy in this exposé is an essay by Charles Richards, "Strength Through Fear" (*Kraft durch Furcht*), a play on the German slogan "Strength Through Joy" (*Kraft durch Freude*). Richards mentioned that Germany was annihilating an entire people, the Jews. The murderers, he said, would be caught. He made a special note of the starvation of children in the Warsaw ghetto and the deportation to the east of four thousand children, separated from their parents, from France. A copy of the pamphlet was intercepted in June 1943 by the German LXXXIV Corps, stationed in an area from Belgian Antwerp to Holland. By that time massive gassing had already taken place in Treblinka, which had swallowed the Warsaw Jews, and Auschwitz, which had received the French Jewish children, but neither destination was mentioned in the essay.[39]

The publications of the underground, together with proclamations, radio broadcasts, and leaflets of the Allied governments, or for that matter the press in the United States, Britain, or neutral countries, all serve to shed light not so much on the events themselves as on the extent of information that was disseminated. These materials are therefore significant not only for what they disclose and criticize but also for what they do not say, either because of ignorance or an unwillingness to publicize what had been discovered.

Unlike open documents, the closed materials encapsulate a confidential process of thought and action, including the ways in which all manner of decisions were made and carried out. They comprise official and personal matters inside and outside the Nazi world, and they are held in archives, manuscript divisions of libraries, and occasionally in private hands.

For the typology of these internal sources, one may differentiate first between circulating documents and those that did not leave someone's desk. Circulation was laid out in Paragraph 38 of the General Code of Administrative Procedures in German Reich Ministries, dated 1928. The directions of the flow are down, sideways, and up, and the corresponding designations of the communications were orders, letters, and reports.[40] As a basic conceptual division, this classification may be applied, with elaborations and refinements, to all correspondence, central or regional, German or non-German,

39. Report of LXXXIV Corps/Ic (Intelligence) for June 1943, dated July 3, 1943, National Archives, Record Group 242, T 314, Roll 1628. The Germans labeled the pamphlet "enemy propaganda."

40. See Arnold Brecht and Comstock Glaser, *The Art and Technique of Administration in German Ministries* (Cambridge, Mass., 1940), p. 69.

civilian or military, governmental or corporate. All these organizations engaged in anti-Jewish actions and all produced
records of their activities and transactions. This pervasiveness
of involvement is revealed in the documents at every turn. A
flag-production company in Berlin manufactured Jewish
stars.[41] The Allianz Insurance Company provided coverage for
forced labor camps in the Lublin and Galician districts of occupied Poland.[42] In Lvov, Galicia, the municipal division responsible for gardening supplied camouflage plants for a local
Jewish labor camp.[43] And in the Bialystok district in Poland, a
detachment of air force personnel, resting in the woods after
the trauma of having been shot down, hunted fleeing and hiding Jews to regain mental stability.[44]

Not only was there a mix of agencies. A communication,
no matter where it was generated, could also contain a variety
of topics. Jews were discussed routinely alongside other subjects; the folders labeled only "Jews" are relatively few. The
documentary sources pertaining to the Jewish catastrophe are
therefore not an immediately identifiable portion of the remaining material. They will be found across and within all
kinds of collections.

Finally one must always keep in mind that the internal correspondence was more than an aggregate of pages. Each piece

41. Memorandum by Paul Eppstein (Jewish Reichsvereinigung in
Berlin), September 20, 1941, Leo Baeck Institute, Microfilm 66.
42. SS Economic-Administrative Main Office/W IV to W IV branch in
Kraków, October 19, 1944, Nuremberg trials document NO-3766 and reply
by Kraków branch, October 25, 1944, NO-3765.
43. Correspondence of September 11, 1943, in Lvov Oblast Archives,
Fond 37, Opis 4, Folder 117. The forced-labor camp (*Zwangsarbeitslager,*
abbr. ZAL) for Jews was in Lvov.
44. Report of the Jägersonderkommando (Hunter Special Detachment)
of the Luftwaffe (Air Force), June 1, 1943, Zentrale Stelle in Ludwigsburg,
Collection Verschiedenes. The commander of the unit was Captain Frevert.

of paper was once an action. It became a concrete step with real consequences in the ongoing process of destruction. Every order had a specific effect on its recipients, enlarging or diminishing their authority or burden. The impact would then be widened as soon as they passed it on to *their* subordinates, until the full brunt of what had been ordered might be felt by the victims. A letter, in turn, was a way of achieving clarity and agreement about an action to be taken. A report, which at first glance is just a record of events, fulfilled two purposes. It confirmed to the leadership the continual functioning of the administrative machine, and provided an overview that was a tool for shaping future decisions.

Orders could be written or unwritten. Those in writing may be discovered, if preserved, within the multitudinous items of correspondence. Oral orders surface, if at all, only when there is a reference to them in documents or testimony.

In Germany a nomenclature existed for written orders. The armed forces, as well as the SS and Police, used the simple word *Befehl*, which has all the connotations of a demand that is unambiguous and not to be questioned. Necessarily, the level at which an order was given was clearly specified, e.g., army, corps, division, and so on. In the concentration camps an order of a camp command was called a *Kommandanturbefehl*. To the extent that orders in the civilian bureaucracy were labeled, the formal headings were

Directive: *Erlass*
   if circulated widely: *Runderlass*
Administrative order: *Verfügung*
   if circulated widely: *Rundverfügung*
Instructions: *Anweisung*[45]

45. Sommerlatte (Riga) to Gebietskommissare, December 7, 1942, National Archives, Record Group 242, T 459, Roll 2.

The Erlass was an instrument of high authority such as Hitler himself, a ministry, or the ruler of a large occupied region. Sometimes Erlasse dealt with fundamental matters, such as those by Hitler for the administration, economy, and police jurisdiction in the newly occupied Soviet territories,[46] but they might address any issue deemed to be of concern, as in the case of a Runderlass of the Interior Ministry for the establishment of bordellos to serve foreign workers, who were forbidden to have relationships with German women.[47] An Erlass, like any order, was either a straightforward command or a delegation of power that enabled a lower-level official to take action within certain limits. A complication could arise when that official used two Erlasse, issued by separate authorities, to construct an empowerment that neither had clearly intended to give him. This happened just before the ration cards of Jews were marked in the whole of Germany, when they were stamped with a "J" in Frankfurt. In the ensuing correspondence, the measure was defended by citing two secret Erlasse (*Geheimerlasse*), one by Minister President Hermann Göring, the other by the Minister of Food and Agriculture.[48]

Verfügungen were usually issued either in pursuance of a published Verordnung (decree) or an Erlass. When the chief of the Warsaw district received 57,000 blank labor registration

46. Texts enclosed in Reich Minister for Eastern Occupied Territories (Alfred Rosenberg) to his offices in the northern region (the Ostland) of the territories, September 3, 1941, German Federal Archives, R 43 II/685.

47. Runderlass of Interior Ministry (signed by Ministerialdirektor Fritz Cropp of the Division for Public Health), October 24, 1942, facsimile in Jochen August, *et al.*, *Herrenmensch und Arbeitsvölker* (Berlin, 1986), pp. 134–135.

48. Food Office in Frankfurt to the Mayor of Frankfurt, March 8, 1940, in Kommission zur Erforschung der Geschichte der Frankfurter Juden, *Dokumente zur Geschichte der Frankfurter Juden 1933–1945* (Frankfurt am Main, 1963), pp. 447–448. See also earlier correspondence on pp. 443–444.

cards from an office of Generalgouverneur Frank, to whom he was subordinate, he wrote a Verfügung requiring the registration of Jewish men for forced labor in the district.[49] Following the regularization of marked ration cards in Germany, a *Dienstanweisung* was used in Frankfurt to list the quantities of food items allowed to Jews for a weekly ration period.[50] Often, however, the term "Anweisung," or its equivalent, the "Dienstanweisung," was simply omitted in communications that were understood as such.

Explanations needed by local offices or units in the field to carry out a particular measure were furnished in guidelines (*Richtlinien*) or in an instruction sheet (*Merkblatt*). Richtlinien were prepared in 1940 by the chief of Security Police, Reinhard Heydrich, for the deportation of Gypsies from western areas of Germany.[51] A Merkblatt was sent by an army lieutenant colonel of a rear-echelon command responsible for a significant section of the occupied Soviet territory to indigenous mayors, instructing them that the Jews were to be told to make and wear a yellow patch.[52]

An important deviation from the formal outlining of mandatory actions was the oral order. For Adolf Hitler it was the principal mode of making his wishes known. In 1935 he

49. City President of Warsaw to Warsaw District Chief, February 16, 1940, noting the Verfügung of February 15 and confirming receipt of the blank cards that were passed on to him.

50. Food Office in Frankfurt Dienstanweisung No. 21, October 23, 1942, in *Dokumente zur Geschichte der Frankfurter Juden*, pp. 453–455. The railways used the term "Anordnung" for internal matters, as in "Fahrplananordnung."

51. See the Richtlinien signed by Heydrich, April 27, 1940, in Henry Friedlander and Sybil Milton, eds., *Archives of the Holocaust*, XXII: Zentrale Stelle der Landesjustizverwaltungen (New York, 1993), pp. 3–6.

52. Merkblatt signed by Lt. Col. Laub of Feldkommandantur 551 to local mayors, September 4, 1941, National Archives, Record Group 242, T 315, Roll 1672.

demanded a Reich citizenship law and a law prohibiting the entry into marriages between Germans and Jews.[53] In a conversation with Himmler a year later he expressed a desire for a legal measure prohibiting Jews from giving their children purely German first names.[54] In 1941 he ordered the military to make room for organs of the SS and Police to "eliminate" Jewish-Bolshevik "chieftains" in the course of the campaign planned against the Soviet Union.[55] Again and again he is said in documents to have vetoed, consented to, or initiated anti-Jewish measures. Among these reported oral orders is the blanket one for the physical annihilation of the European Jews.[56] There is also an oblique mention of his wish in early 1943 that the delayed construction projects in Auschwitz—with specific reference to the unfinished gas chambers there—be completed as rapidly as possible.[57] During a visit by Slovak president Josef Tiso in May 1944, Hitler told him with respect to the remaining Jews in Slovakia that now one had to move against them.[58]

53. Affidavit by Bernhard Lösener, February 24, 1948, Nuremberg trials document NG-1944-A.

54. Himmler to Staatssekretär Hans Pfundtner of the Interior Ministry, June 15, 1936, Zentralarchiv (Central Archives of the German Democratic Republic) Potsdam, Collection 15.01 RMdI 27401. These archives were incorporated into the German Federal Archives.

55. Percy Schramm and Hans-Adolf Jacobsen, eds., *Kriegstagebuch des Oberkommandos der Wehrmacht, Wehrmachtführungsstab 1940–1945* (Frankfurt am Main, 1965), I, 340–342.

56. Adolf Eichmann, *Ich, Adolf Eichmann* (Leoni am Starnberger See, 1980), pp. 178–179, 229–230. This book is an edited version of his recollections taped in Argentina.

57. Hauptsturmführer Karl Bischoff (Auschwitz) to Hans Kammler, January 27, 1943, United States Holocaust Memorial Museum Archives, Record Group 11.001 (Center for the Preservation of Documentary Historical Collections, Moscow), Roll 20, Fond 502, Opis 1, Folder 28.

58. Hauptsturmführer Böhrsch (Security Service) to Reich Security Main Office III-B (Hans Ehlich), March 19, 1944, National Archives, Record Group 242, T 175, Roll 583.

The war years in particular were a time when oral orders became the preferred vehicle for inaugurating drastic measures. The police organs that were to move with the army into the Soviet Union, known as *Einsatzgruppen* of the Security Police, were assembled just before the onset of the operation to be informed in somewhat vague speeches and pronouncements about their mission.[59] A lieutenant of the Order Police, Franz Stangl, came face to face with the SS and Police Leader of the Lublin district, Odilo Globocnik, who had organized three annihilation camps. Globocnik installed Stangl as commander of the Sobibór, giving him an explanation on a park bench.[60]

Oral orders were almost standard when the SS and Police had jurisdiction over Jewish councils. When instructions were given to acquire Jewish assets and property for the needs of the SS or for the expenses of deportations, the avoidance of writing could be an off-the-books method of self-help in violation of budgetary procedures.[61] Occasionally this method was an incursion into a rock-hard law, like the one that prohibited abortions. The SS and Police actually ordered them in several instances. Word to that effect was passed to the Jews of Vienna[62] and to the ghetto of Theresienstadt.[63] An *Ein-*

59. Affidavit by Wilhelm Förster, October 23, 1947, Nuremberg trials document NO-5520, and affidavit by Robert Barth, September 17, 1947, NO-4992.

60. Gitta Sereny, *Into That Darkness* (New York, 1974), pp. 101–114. The incident was recounted by Stangl.

61. See Ministerialrat Walter Maedel to Ministrialdirigent Richard Kallenbach (both in Finance Ministry), December 14, 1942, German Federal Archives, R 2/12222

62. Viktor Frankl, *Was nicht in meinen Büchern steht* (Munich, 1995), pp. 65–66. Frankl mentions an "ukase" that was "passed around," but identifies it no further.

63. Saul Friedman, ed., *The Theresienstadt Diary of Gonda Redlich* (Lexington, Ky., 1992), entries of June 19–21, 1943, and June 14, 1944, pp. 126, 147–148.

satzkommando of Einsatzgruppe A in Lithuania noted in the winter of 1941–1942 that Jewish councils in its area had been told orally that any propagation was undesirable, that pregnant Jewish women would have to reckon with "liquidation," but that the Security Police would not pursue Jews for abortion offenses.[64] At that point mass shooting had already occurred, and the remnant ghetto of Vilnius in the Lithuanian district housed in the main only healthy young people, who were employed as laborers. In a period of twelve not fully contiguous months of 1942 and 1943, the Jewish council in that ghetto reported 541 surgical procedures, of which 369 were abortions.[65]

The SS and Police, the military, and civilian agencies alike resorted routinely to oral communications with the Jewish councils. Frequent personal contacts between German overseers and Jewish leaders are apparent in the minutes of the *Reichsvereinigung*, which was the council for the German Jews, and in the private diary of Adam Czerniaków, the chairman of the Jewish council in Warsaw.[66] When the time arrived for mass deportations from the Warsaw ghetto, a special SS "resettlement staff" stepped into Czerniaków's office and bluntly told him that the operation was to begin immediately.[67] Shortly thereafter, council members and the ghetto's chief li-

64. Undated, unsigned report of Einsatzkommando 3 (December 1941–January 1942), Latvian State Archives, Fond 1026, Opis 1, Folder 3.

65. Compiled in a tabulation by Wolfgang Benz, Konrad Kwiet, and Jürgen Matthäus, eds., *Einsatz im "Reichskommissariat Ostland"* (Berlin, 1998), pp. 219–220.

66. Reichsvereinigung Protokolle and other documents pertaining to deportations of German Jews, in Zentralarchiv (Central Archives of the German Democratic Republic) Potsdam, Collection Reichsvereinigung 75c Re 1. Raul Hilberg, Stanislaw Staron, and Josef Kermisz, eds., *The Warsaw Diary of Adam Czerniakow* (New York, 1979), *passim*.

67. Hilberg, *et al.*, *Warsaw Diary of Adam Czerniakow*, entry of July 22, 1942, pp. 384–385.

brarian for the community's Archives and Records Office, Hillel Seidman, went to see the chairman. This is how Seidman describes the meeting in his diary:

> I enter Czerniakow's boardroom. One look at him was enough—the chalk white face, shaking hands, and staring eyes that see nothing. Around him sit a few *Judenrat* [Jewish council] members. Finally Czerniakow notices me and points to a scrap of paper on his desk. "Is there no official notice?" I ask. "No," comes the reply. "This is all there is."
>
> I recognize Czerniakow's writing and begin to read, the letters dancing before my eyes. Later I made a copy for the archives.[68]

The next day Czerniaków killed himself. The librarian had a subsequent meeting with a Gestapo officer, Karl-Georg Brandt, who seemed to be in a relaxed mood. *"Die Organisation klappt, 7000 täglich* [The organization is working well, 7000 daily]," he said.[69]

Written orders were far fewer than oral ones, and letters were outnumbered by conversations. Under Paragraph 38 of the Administrative Code, a formal letter from one official to another of equal standing was called a *Schreiben*, or "writing." The Schreiben, like the order, was a regular form of communication at all levels except the lowest. The content need not have been momentous. A typical example is a letter by a local German official, the Kreishauptmann in Częstochowa, Richard Wendler, to his military counterpart, the Stadtkommandant, requesting that soldiers not walk around in the

68. Hillel Seidman, *The Warsaw Ghetto Diaries* (Southfield, Mich., 1997), entry of July 22, 1942, pp. 52–53.
69. *Ibid.*, entry of July 24, 1942, p. 63. The translator's German spelling is corrected here.

ghetto.[70] Conversations between officials in person or by telephone were seldom recorded verbatim. Formal meetings were, however, summarized. A conversation between two or three officials was usually called a *Rücksprache*, and a period meeting was a *Besprechung*. A conference summary was a *Niederschrift*, but in the Jewish community in Berlin, a synopsis of the discussion was a *Protokoll*.[71]

A formal agreement that settled an issue was officially a *Vereinbarung*. Its terms could be contained in a letter from one agency to another, such as that of the SS and Police Leader in Galicia providing for the retention, after the onset of deportations, of Jews needed for war production by the army's armament command in the area,[72] or that of the Justice Ministry containing the friendly transfer of its criminal jurisdiction over Jews and Gypsies to the SS and Police.[73]

A contract between two companies, as in a takeover of a Jewish firm by a German one, was simply a *Vertrag*, irrespective of the pressure felt by the Jewish seller. Fraudulent contracts between the SS and elderly Jews about to be sent to Theresienstadt, promising the prospective deportees accommodations in the ghetto in exchange for their money, were called *Heimeinkaufvertäge*, or "home purchase contracts."[74]

70. Wendler to Stadtkommandantur, April 25, 1941, Yad Vashem Microfilm JM 1489.

71. See Zentralarchiv (Central Archives of the German Democratic Republic) Potsdam, Collection Reichsvereinigung 75c Re 1, Laufende Nummer 2.

72. SS and Police Leader Fritz Katzmann to Armament Command in Lvov, October 23, 1942, in Katzmann's report about the deportations in his area, June 20, 1943, Nuremberg trials document L-18.

73. Memorandum by Justice Minister Otto Thierack, September 18, 1942, Nuremberg trials document PS-654.

74. For the text of a takeover contract involving J. & C. A. Schneider Company of Frankfurt, December 27, 1938, see National Archives, Record Group 242, T 83, Roll 97. A facsimile of a Heimeinkaufvertrag is in Adler,

The SS also made regular contracts with German firms that received concentration camp labor.[75]

Extant private letters are for the most part isolated fragments. Now and then one may find a personal letter from one official to another. Staatsrat Harald Turner in Serbia sent such a letter to an SS acquaintance, expressing exhilaration about actions against the Jews.[76] Soldiers' letters to their families, read by censors, still exist in modest quantities.[77] Letters of Jewish deportees from Germany in occupied Poland before the onset of killing operations contain glimpses of life in the new surroundings.[78] Letters from a Jewish woman in a miniprison to her half-Jewish children were smuggled out and saved.[79] The briefest messages from Jews may be found on postcards from internment and concentration camps. Necessarily they had to be bland.[80]

The largest segment of all communications consisted of reports. The term in the Administrative Code for a written re-

Die verheimlichte Wahrheit, pp. 55–56. See also Collection Reichsvereinigung of the Zentralarchiv (Central Archives of the German Democratic Republic) Potsdam, 75c Re 1, Laufende Nummern 522–552.

75. For example, a contract between the SS Economic-Administrative Main Office/Office Group D and the Ostmaschinenbau GmbH., April 26, 1944, for renting fourteen hundred Auschwitz inmates at set rates of hourly compensation payable to the SS. Facsimile in Franciszek Piper, *Arbeitseinsatz der Häftlinge aus dem KL Auschwitz* (Oświęcim, Poland, 1995), glossy unnumbered pages.

76. Turner to Richard Hildebrandt, October 17, 1941, Nuremberg trials document NO-5810.

77. Excerpts in Walter Manoschek, *"Es gibt nur eines für das Judentum: Vernichtung"* (Hamburg, 1995).

78. Texts in Else Behrend-Rosenfeld and Gertrud Luckner, eds., *Lebenszeichen aus Piaski* (Munich, 1970).

79. For example, the letters written from Breitenau by Lilli Jahn, a Jewish physician who was separated from her non-Jewish husband, in Gunnar Richter, ed., *Breitenau* (Kassel, 1993), p. 294, n207. The letters were written to her children. She was deported to Auschwitz, where she died.

80. Facsimiles in Schwab, *Echoes, passim.*

port was *Bericht*. When ranking officials reported in person to a higher authority, their presentation was called a *Vortrag*. For example, the Chief of the Reich Chancellery, which acted as a clearinghouse for matters that might have to be brought to the attention of Hitler, would ask the Führer directly whether one-quarter Jews should be deprived of their agricultural properties. He then communicated the answer, which was "no," in writing to the Minister of Agriculture.[81]

Reports, which might include questions or suggestions, were made in every organization. They could be daily, weekly, biweekly, monthly, or annual. There were summary reports about operations that, while still in progress, had been going on for months, such as the recapitulation by Einsatzgruppe A of its activities and experiences from June 22 to October 15, 1941.[82] Final reports were made of a completed action, as exemplified by the elaborate document submitted by the SS and Police Leader in Warsaw after he had completed the three-week sweep of the remnant ghetto, where he had encountered Jewish resistance.[83]

The whole of the reporting system was a pyramid in which the lowest level produced the largest volume. Reports were so ubiquitous that despite massive losses of records due to deliberate or accidental destruction, the remaining pieces furnish a great deal of what may be learned. It is in the reports where some of the missing orders are mentioned, and where most of the places, dates, and numbers are found. This generalization

81. Hans Lammers (Reich Chancellery) to Walter Darré (Minister of Agriculture), April 10, 1941, in Friedlander and Milton, *Archives of the Holocaust*, vol. 20: German National Archives, pp. 32–33.

82. Report by Einsatzgruppe A, October 15, 1941, Nuremberg trials document L-18.

83. Jürgen Stroop to the Higher SS and Police Leader in the General-gouvernement (Poland), Friedrich Krüger, May 16, 1943, Nuremberg trials document PS-1061.

applies also to the reports of Jewish councils from which the German overseers wanted all kinds of information.

Not all documents were circulating. It was routine for officials to make notes to themselves: the *Vermerk* or *Aktennotiz*. Also stationary were folders kept in personnel offices about individuals. Although most were not bulky, some contain—in addition to a photograph, personal background data, assignments, evaluations, and promotions—letters, notes of incidents, and disciplinary actions which can fill several hundred pages.[84] Larger still were the official diaries. The *Diensttagebuch* of the Generalgouverneur in Poland, Hans Frank, consists of many volumes. They are filled with his speeches, summaries of meetings, notations about receptions, inspection trips, and more.[85] The military *Kriegstagebuch* was the chronological log of a unit such as a division, and includes not only entries of daily events but also reports of constituent elements, like the regiments of the division.

A sizable portion of the private diaries was produced by Jews who had special motivations to write them. The Jewish authors might well be presumed to have thought about an eventual dissemination of their observations and experiences, either in the form of a memoir based on their notes, or the publication of the diary itself. At the least they must have considered the possibility of its preservation in an archives, a library, or by their family. Yet the diaries still in existence are probably a small fraction of the original number. If a discovered manuscript is the work of someone who did not survive, there may have been a chain of possessors, and the recovered pages may be incomplete. Those pages, however, are likely to

84. For example, the file of Fritz Katzmann, Berlin Document Center. The center was turned over to the German Federal Archives.

85. See National Archives, Record Group 238, T 992. In the microfilmed diary, which fills twelve rolls, some parts are missing.

be pristine, particularly if the writer of them had no time for revisions. Joseph Goebbels, Adam Czerniaków, and the French Jewish leader Raymond-Raoul Lambert are all diarists whose death occurred in wartime, and their diaries are key documents.[86]

What did the signatory of an internal document think about the afterlife of his order, letter, report, or memorandum? Would it not be dangerous for such an item to fall into the hands of outsiders in some postwar year? Yet at the height of the operation, well before its end, some German bureaucrats and even Jewish functionaries harbored the idea that the mounds of paper on their desks were historic, that without this evidence of their lives and activities, oblivion might overtake them too. In a Dortmund archives, the historian Konrad Kwiet found a recapitulation, written by the director of the municipal pawnshop in August 1941, of gold and silver objects taken from Jews in 1939. The document concludes with the following sentence:

> If even in later years a researcher who is acquainted with Jews only through hearsay, would rummage in the records of the municipal archives of Dortmund, he will discover that the municipal pawnshops also did their small part in the solution of the Jewish question.[87]

In the Łódź ghetto, the Jewish "Self-Administration" created an office for "resettlers" (*Eingesiedelten*) in November

86. Joseph Goebbels, *Die Tagebücher* (Munich, 1987, 1993, and 1996), 20 vols. Hilberg, *et al.*, *The Warsaw Diary of Adam Czerniakow*, and in the original Polish: Marian Fuks, ed., *Adama Czerniakowa dziennik getta warszawskiego*, 2nd ed. (Warsaw, 1983). Raymond-Raoul Lambert, *Carnet d'un témoin*, ed. Richard Cohen (Paris, 1985).

87. Excerpt of the document reprinted in Konrad Kwiet, "Nach dem Pogrom: Stufen der Ausgrenzung," in Wolfgang Benz, ed., *Die Juden in Deutschland 1933–1945* (Munich, 1993), pp. 564–565.

1941 to provide space for deportees from Germany and sur-rounding small ghettos. The writers of the Łódź ghetto chronicle noted on December 6, 1942, after the large majority of the new "settlers" had been placed on transports to be gassed, that the office had to be disbanded. The concluding sentence of the paragraph reads: "Of course, this office will have major significance in the history of the ghetto."[88]

Accounts were rendered after the end of the Nazi regime by perpetrators, onlookers, and survivors. Just as these rendi-tions, in whatever form, may be labeled "testimony," the per-sons who testified may be called witnesses.

Testimony is highly varied and widely scattered. The sim-plest way of segmenting it by type is to relate it to a forum. In this manner, four categories emerge:

Legal testimony
Interviews of specific persons
Oral history
Memoir literature

The legal venue is a matter of place or the receiving ad-dress. It stems from a requirement of proof to arrive at a court judgment, or to sustain a legal claim before an administrative body. An interview is sought by an author or researcher to ob-tain information for a delimited purpose. Oral history is a col-lection of open-ended accounts from witnesses, with a view to preservation and possible use at a later time by other persons. The memoir is intended to stand alone. It may be passed on to family and friends, or deposited somewhere to be stored, or published as an essay or book.

88. Danuta Dabrowska and Lucjan Dobroszycki, eds., *Kronika getta łódzkiego* (Łódź, 1965), II, 573.

In the legal framework, testimony is hemmed in. It must be relevant to the case or claim, with due allowance for the personal background of the witness and room for questions about awareness, intent, and habitual behavior. The extent, moreover, of what is admissible or demanded may be determined by the kind of judicial or administrative proceeding. There were war crimes trials under international or national jurisdiction; murder trials in the Federal Republic of Germany; treason trials in eastern Europe; denaturalization and deportation trials in the United States; extradition trials in various countries; libel suits, property suits, and, in the United States, class-action suits; and indemnification and restitution proceedings reviewable in the German Federal Republic by special administrative courts. The nature of all this testimony is structured not only by the type of proceeding but by applicable laws of evidence that differ from country to country.

Trials were held and claims were pursued from the end of the war to the beginning of the twenty-first century. In the late 1940s the aged but lucid former Hungarian regent, Admiral Miklos Horthy, was a witness in a Nuremberg case, describing the German takeover of Hungary in March 1944 and its consequences.[89] Fifty years later claims forms were filled out by eighty-year-old people for shares of a settlement obtained from Swiss banks.[90] No overall count has been made

89. See his testimony in Nuremberg subsequent trials, U.S. v. Weizsäcker, *et al.* (Case No. 11), English transcript pp. 2701–2747.

90. Clyde Haberman, "Swiss Offer Is Another Test for Holocaust Survivor," *New York Times*, October 15, 1999, p. A29. Reportedly 550,000 questionnaires had been returned as of May 2000 by survivors or their heirs under the agreement, which covered not only bank accounts but wages lost by forced laborers of Swiss companies or of companies with Swiss accounts, and indemnities to fleeing victims who had been turned back at the Swiss border by Swiss authorities. The statistic is in Alan Feuer, "Final Approval on Swiss Holocaust Claims," *New York Times*, July 27, 2000, p. A8.

and no overview has been attempted of all these statements and forms.

By contrast, comparatively few authors and filmmakers created their own source base by contacting witnesses for answers to specific questions. The subject of their interest might have been an event, institution, locality, or even the interviewed person. The assembled information would then be distilled for the dimensions of a book or film. In this way Gitta Sereny prepared a biography of Franz Stangl, the commander of Sobibór and, subsequently, Treblinka.[91] John K. Dickinson concentrated on a single Jewish victim who was not a public figure and who had perished. To trace the life of this man, Dickinson questioned 172 persons, most of them Germans.[92] Gordon Horwitz studied the population that lived in the vicinity of the former concentration camp Mauthausen, and interviewed some of these local Austrian bystanders at length.[93] Claude Lanzmann fashioned a panoramic film, *Shoah*, for which he contacted many individuals, most of them simple people in small places. Deliberately he introduced no documentary footage of World War II, so that, with his own pictures and sound, the questions and answers, cut down as if chiseled, became the content of the nine-and-a-half-hour film.[94]

In oral history collections, the witnesses are in the main survivors. Perpetrators are absent, and with rare exceptions even the close non-Jewish neighbors of the destroyed commu-

91. Sereny, *Into That Darkness.*
92. John K. Dickinson, *German and Jew* (Chicago, 1967).
93. Gordon J. Horwitz, *In the Shadow of Death* (New York, 1990).
94. *Shoah* (Paris, 1985), on tape with English subtitles, Paramount Home Video (1985), VHS 2395. In book form in French, allotting only one line for each subtitle of the film (Paris, 1985), and in English, with subtitles running into each other (New York, 1985).

nities are not represented. The organizers of these projects were Jews who were preoccupied with the Jewish fate and with the manner in which that history should be presented to the public. They were convinced that survivors would speak with the deepest knowledge and that they were the most trustworthy.

Two peaks were reached in the gathering of oral history information. The first encompasses the years from 1944 to about 1948, before most of the survivors had left Europe. Statements were collected in newly liberated France, Poland, and Soviet territories. In succeeding years material was still gathered in Tel Aviv, Israel, where passersby walked into an unobtrusive office and told their stories on tape recorders. The staff in Tel Aviv consisted of survivors who were of the same age as the witnesses, and who had themselves had the kinds of experiences that were related in the accounts.[95]

The second surge of oral history occurred in the 1980s and 1990s. Now the concern was that the survivors would die off soon, and that a concerted effort was required to interview all of them. The epitome of this undertaking was a computerized video archives begun by the filmmaker Steven Spielberg. Some fifty thousand people were interviewed, but neither by their contemporaries nor by experts. The questioners could have been grandchildren of the witnesses, and the hasty preparation of the staff was not always sufficient for an adequate familiarity with the subject.[96]

95. The director was Rachel Auerbach, a Warsaw ghetto survivor and wartime associate of the chronicler Emanuel Ringelblum.

96. See Peter Gumbel, "Making History," *Wall Street Journal*, March 2, 1999, p. R9, and Henryk Broder, "Indiana Jones in Auschwitz," *Der Spiegel*, September 13, 1999, pp. 246–264. More modest projects were conducted over a longer period by the Yale Video Archives and the United States Holocaust Memorial Museum. Yad Vashem continued in Israel.

Notwithstanding the quantity of words in oral history, it is inherently limited in three respects: (1) The survivors as a whole are not a random sample of the Jewish community that was destroyed. (2) Those who testified are not a random sample of the survivors. (3) Their testimony does not contain a random sample of their experiences.

Point one is basic. Survivors as a group differ in their physical makeup, social background, and psychological traits from the population that was annihilated. The physical advantages for survival were youth, strength, and health. In the societal domain, the favorable factors were a mixed marriage, protected foreign nationality, prominence, recognized skills, and financial resources. In threatening situations, one's chances were enhanced by such behavioral characteristics as realistic thinking, rapid decision-making, self-reliance, and sheer tenacity. On average, all these elements were present among survivors to a far greater extent than in the mass that succumbed to the assault.

The witnesses are not a cross section of the survivors, because they do not include men and women who volunteered nothing. The abstainers might have harmed other victims. They could have shied away from recalling instances of weakness, helplessness, or humiliation. Alternatively they could have concluded that they did not have enough to say if they had not been in Auschwitz for some time, or if they had not jumped from a moving train, or if they had not joined a partisan unit in the woods. Many could have been apathetic because they thought their entire life was barren and unfulfilled.

The testimony that is related may be far from an all-encompassing account. The choice of topics, whether in a statement prepared by the survivor or in an interview, was determined not only by readiness or reluctance to delve into particular episodes but by a perception of what was or was not pertinent information. Details, however harmless, might not have surfaced if one could not foresee what someone might look for in the testimony. By the same token, accounts could be very similar in substance, particularly if a number of surviving witnesses testified about a common experience in a specific place.[97]

Like the materials in the oral history depots, the published memoirs appeared in two waves, the first just after the war and the second at the end of the century. The limits and limitations of oral delivery apply also to books, and on occasion even more so. The authors had to make themselves available. They had to invest their time and step forward with an idea, outline, draft, or manuscript. What they finally offered remained a personal account with selected revelations.

97. Christopher Browning found such a "firm core of shared memory" in 134 accounts of survivors who were in the labor camps of Starachowice. See his *Nazi Policy, Jewish Workers, German Killers* (Cambridge, England, 2000), pp. 90–92. Browning estimates that the camps held 2,300 Jewish inmates.

TWO

Composition

◻ The structure of the sources is a kind of organized space. In pictorial representations, the contents were selected and shown as found or arranged within a frame. In architecture, the process began with design. In the written materials, the information was ordered on a page and the pages were organized in a collection. In every case the modes and characteristics of composition were anchored in a pre-Nazi era. They had been solidified in countless replications and were put to use like an inheritance for a new purpose.

Beginning with photography, one might look at two bearded men who had just arrived in Auschwitz. The portrait was prepared indoors, with obvious deliberation, by the SS photographic staff in the camp.[1] Neither the typification nor the pose was new. An example of a precursor is the bearded

1. See Peter Hellman, *The Auschwitz Album* (New York, 1981), p. 3. The deportees, from Greater Hungary, came in 1944.

man in a fresco painted by Fra Angelico in the early 1400s, when profiles bathed in light were already in vogue.[2]

The architectural blueprints for the gas chambers in Auschwitz-Birkenau are similarly connected with the past. They were the work of draftsmen who might have designed any building before or after the war. One must peer at the Auschwitz drawings closely to see that they are not ordinary. The first of them was in fact only that of a mortuary with ovens for cremation. This familiar facility was subsequently modified so that a gas chamber would replace the storage room for bodies.[3]

A similar adjustment, this time in the realm of law, appears in the text of a tax measure. In 1931 a property tax had been devised, payable by prospective emigrants. In 1934 the due percentage amounts were simply increased in an amendment without so much as a reference to the new objective of targeting the emigrating Jews.[4]

The whole of the voluminous internal correspondence produced by the bureaucracy also conformed to established patterns. It was fashioned in time-honored ways and transmitted through channels hollowed out by generations of functionaries. Formats were adopted and adapted during the Nazi period. Even the testimony of survivors was not a novel medium of communication. An attempt to record Jewish experiences in times of persecution had already been made rudimentarily in 1903, when a young poet of the Hebrew lan-

---

2. Fra Angelico's fresco is in the Dominican convent of San Marco in Florence. See Paolo Morachiello, *Fra Angelico—The San Marco Frescoes* (London, 1996), illustration on unnumbered page. For the dating, see John T. Spike, *Fra Angelico* (New York, 1997), pp. 71–73.

3. Jean-Claude Pressac, *Auschwitz: Technique and Operation of the Gas Chambers* (New York, 1989), pp. 183–184, 284–303, 355–378.

4. For 1931, see RGBl I, 699, 731–733; for 1934, RGBl I, 392.

Two bearded men from Hungary who had just arrived in Auschwitz in 1944. The portrait was prepared by the SS photographic staff in the camp.

A bearded man in a fresco painted by Fra Angelico in the early 1400s.

guage, Haym Nahum Bialyk, was dispatched to collect eyewitness accounts after a pogrom in Kishinev.[5] Again, on a much larger scale, a British team during World War I gathered information from Armenians who had been driven from their homes and who had evaded death on their trek from the eastern provinces of the Ottoman Empire.[6]

The linear descent of Holocaust sources from preexisting models is therefore pervasive. It is manifest in every artifact and every piece of paper. Seldom is there any deviation from usage. In the creation and distribution of documents, form follows form, and routine perpetuates routine. In testimony, storytelling reveals its ancient components.

Standardization was a veritable hallmark of official German correspondence. The old rules and practices were applied to signatures, layouts, routing, and filing. This system was more than a formality; it constituted the essence of everything that was considered orderly procedure. The ingrained order was preserved whenever anything was written.

Communications were deeply embedded in the hierarchical character of an agency. Under a minister, the highest officeholder was a *Staatssekretär*, who supervised all or several of the ministry's activities. A ministry was divided into *Abteilungen*, each headed by a *Ministerialdirektor*. If an Abteilung was divided into *Unterabteilungen* or *Gruppen*, the Ministrialdirektor's immediate subordinate was a *Ministerialdirigent*. The next lower level, either directly under an Abteilung or an Unterabteilung, was the *Referat*, a more specialized unit headed by a *Referent*. In a ministry this official had the title of *Ministerial-*

5. David G. Roskies, *The Jewish Search for a Usable Past* (Bloomington, Ind., 1999), p. 18.
6. Viscount Bryce, Documents presented to Viscount Grey of Fallodon, *The Treatment of Armenians* (London, 1916). The report was prepared by Arnold Toynbee.

rat. Some Ministerialräte, or their assistants, became specialists in Jewish affairs. In the regional network of a ministry, an expert would be a *Regierungsrat.*[7] In cities the term *Dezernat* was used instead of Referat, and the municipal specialist was a *Dezernent,* who might also have been preoccupied with Jewish affairs. The names of all these officeholders, and in many cases also those of functionaries serving under them, regularly appear in the documents.

Special refinements were cultivated in the matter of signatures. They could be handwritten (and virtually illegible), without the typed name underneath. Sometimes initials were offered, with the last name typed in parentheses. If a final text was previously initialed in draft form by the sender, the last name would usually be spelled out in type, occasionally preceded by the lettering *Gez.* (*gezeichnet*—signed). For authentication, the signature of a subordinate would be appended with the notation *f.d.R.* (*für die Richtigkeit*) or *beglaubigt,* both meaning "certified as correct." The same method was used for typewritten copies of a communication.

Signing was raised to a refined craft when the authority of an administrative or military organization was invoked by a member of its staff or the head of one of its subunits. In that instance the signer claimed to represent a superior. Generally the organization would be identified on a letterhead and the position of the signer would be indicated in the top left corner in an added abbreviation. But that was not enough. In a ministry the signer below the rank of minister would also place an *i.V.* or an *i.A.* above his signature. The i.V. stood for *in Vertretung* (deputizing) and the i.A. for *im Auftrag* (by instruction). In the code of 1928, the Staatssekretär would use the i.V. for the type of communication not usually signed by the minister.

7. In the Foreign Office the rank of Botschaftsrat was used instead of Ministerialrat, and Gesandtschaftsrat instead of Regierungsrat.

A Ministerialdirektor would sign a document when the signature had not been reserved by the Staatssekretär for himself, but only with an i.A. A Ministerialrat had to have specific authorization to sign such documents, and then he too was limited to an i.A.

The system of the i.V. and i.A. was extended to the field. The name of a major of the Order Police, who was the operations officer on the staff of the Commander (*Kommandeur*) of the Order Police in the Byelorussian region (in German: Weissruthenien), appears in the signature line of an order by the Kommandeur, dated August 14, 1943, with the symbol i.V. That order had a provision of how one could and could not refer to the "Jewish Question."[8] If an official in the agricultural office of the Generalkommissar for Byelorussia wrote to the agricultural section of the Gebietskommissar of Baranowicze (a subregion in Byelorussia), setting rations (bread, potatoes, and warm soup daily) for Jewish workers assigned to road building, he did so with an i.A.[9] Again, a staff member in the office of the Kommissar of the Warsaw ghetto signed a measure dealing with ghetto boundaries with an i.A.[10] So did

8. Kommandeur of Order Police in Byelorussia, Order No. 17, August 14, 1943, with typed signature of Major Kurth. United States Holocaust Memorial Museum Archives, Record Group 53.002 (Belarus Central Archives), Roll 3, Fond 389, Opis 1, Folder 1. The order stated that there was to be no public discussion of a "total solution" (*Gesamtlösung*), but group allocation of Jewish labor could be mentioned.

9. Generalkommissar/Agriculture III (signature illegible) to Gebietskommissar in Baranowicze, February 9, 1942, *ibid.*, Roll 4, Fond 393, Opis 3, Folder 16. The signer had the rank of Kriegsverwaltungsrat.

10. Probst to Czerniaków, December 6, 1941, Yad Vashem Archives, Microfilm JM 1112. Probst signed only with his initials. In the left-hand corner appear the typed letters "Pro/Mo." Pro is Hermann Probst and Mo is Friedel Mohr. Both were considered employees (*Gefolgschaft*) in Kommissar Heinz Auerswald's office. See the list, consisting of nine names, as of December 4, 1941, *ibid.* Auerswald was subordinated to Gouverneur Ludwig Fischer, who reported to Hans Frank.

Fanny Czarna, when she signed an urgent order, dated December 29, 1941, of a member of the Jewish directorate of community councils in Eastern Upper Silesia, Chaim Merin, instructing the councils to collect all the ski equipment, including boots and socks, from Jews in the area, for delivery to German agencies.[11]

Complications could arise, however, if a signer dispensed with these symbols altogether, or if he used them without a prior grant of authority. The Reichskommissar of the Ostland, whose domain included the Baltic and Byelorussian areas, informed his Generalkommissar in Byelorussia that the SS and Police Leader in Byelorussia was not an independent agent but a deputy of the Generalkommissar in police matters. If, therefore, the Generalkommissar was absent, the SS and Police Leader was expected to sign as the "Generalkommissar in Vertretung" whenever anything except the internal business of the SS and Police was involved. If the SS and Police Leader was absent, his subordinate was to sign such items as the "Generalkommissar im Auftrag."[12] To be sure, the insistence of territorial civil authorities on the subordination of the SS and Police was a losing proposition.

In Berlin, Adolf Eichmann overstepped a much clearer boundary when he signed a directive "i.A." in the absence of the Gestapo chief Heinrich Müller, without having sought permission from a deputy of Müller. In that situation the "i.A." was an arrogation of power, especially because the communication was sent to regional officers who were higher in rank than Eichmann. Müller subsequently expressed his dis-

11. Czarna to councils, December 29, 1941, United States Holocaust Memorial Museum Archives, Record Group 15.061 (Jewish Interest Representation [a regional council] of Bendsburg [Będzyn], Roll 1.

12. Reichskommissar Ostland II/Administration, signed [Hinrich] Lohse, to Generalkommissar in Minsk, December 5, 1942, National Archives, Record Group 242, T 459, Roll 22.

pleasure to Eichmann, but the two men were on good terms and by then Eichmann had become indispensable.[13]

Many items were part of a sequence. If a letter introduced a new subject, a note in the vicinity of the salutation would be made that there was no preceding correspondence (*Vorgang: ohne*). In a continuing exchange, the word *Bezug* (reference) was used to identify the prior item, and *Betreff* (abbr. *Betr.*) would be added with a word or phrase describing the topic.

Orders given for a short duration, particularly to uniformed personnel, would sometimes be numbered consecutively. This was the habit of the military commander in Byelorussia,[14] the commander of a Lithuanian police battalion,[15] and the commandant of Auschwitz.[16] The Jewish Reichsvereinigung in Berlin numbered the protocols of its meetings.[17] The Einsatzgruppen of the Security Police in the occupied USSR sent their reports to Berlin, where they were consolidated for distribution and numbered on a daily basis.[18] When a report covered events over a span of time, the opening and closing dates would be indicated.

The structure of documents was taken from patterns of old: numbered articles in laws and decrees; subheadings in reports; dates in diaries. If there was nothing to report under a

13. Eichmann, *Ich*, pp. 148–149.

14. See the orders (1941) in United States Holocaust Memorial Museum Archives, Record Group 53.002 (Belarus Central Archives), Roll 2, Fond 378, Opis 1, Folder 69.

15. See the orders of the 2nd Battalion (1941) in Lithuanian Central Archives, Fond 1444, Opis 1, Folder 3.

16. See Norbert Frei, et al., *Standort– und Kommandanturbefehle des Konzentrationslagers Auschwitz 1940–1945* (Munich, 2000). Both the Standortbefehle and the Kommandanturbefehle, the texts of which are reproduced in Frei's volume, were numbered consecutively by year. Special orders in each category (*Sonderbefehle*) were not numbered.

17. See Leo Baeck Institute, Microfilm Roll 66.

18. See Helmut Krausnick and Hans-Heinrich Wilhelm, *Die Truppe des Weltanschauungskrieges* (Stuttgart, 1981), pp. 649–654.

given subheading, the word *Fehlanzeige* (nil) would be inserted. In the Volhynian marshes during the summer of 1941, where Police Regiment Center was engaged in unprecedented activities, the commander, Max Montua, specified what he wanted to know in a band of headings:[19]

Time	Place	Prisoners taken		Shootings		
Zeit	*Ort*	*eingebrachte Gefangene*		*Erschiessungen*		
		Russian soldiers	Jews	Women	Reason	
		russische Soldaten	*Juden*	*Frauen*	*Grund*	

The categories in this order are highly revealing. Although the regiment had already shot Jewish men, the killing had not yet encompassed the Jewish women and children. The uncertainty in the field mirrored thoughts in the higher echelons, still evolving, about annihilating the Jews. Reasons were still needed, if only pro forma. Equally important, however, was the requirement of uniform reporting by the battalions. The statistics that each of them was required to furnish had to be combined by the regimental staff without the difficulty of incompatible categories or undecipherable obfuscation. Finally, the essential information was to be formulated as briefly as possible. It was not to be drowned in long paragraphs.

Brevity was also a necessity in war diaries. Long reports could be appended to daily entries, but the descriptions under a date had to be limited to essentials, without elaborate explanations. Paragraphs were consequently short and adjectives

19. Order by Police Regiment Center, July 27, 1941, Military Historical Archives, Prague, Collection SS-Polizei Regiment A 3-1-7/2, K. 1.

generally omitted. The result was a density of facts. The following item, from the 1944 diary of the Armament Command in Radom, is typical:

April 15, 1944

During the night from 15 to 16, 4 the Tatar Guard fled from station C of Hasag Kamienna, taking along an MG, three MPs, rifles and 60 rounds of ammunition.[20]

The Tatars were collaborators. Station C was in section C of the Jewish labor camp at Skarżysko-Kamienna. Hasag was a German company, Hugo Schneider A.G., with headquarters in Leipzig and branches in labor camps. The MG was a machine gun and the MPs machine pistols (submachine guns in American idiom).

Adam Czerniaków, the chairman of the Jewish Council in the Warsaw ghetto, kept a personal diary in notebooks small enough to fit into an inside coat pocket. Although he wrote passages about his private doubts and anxieties, he devoted the bulk of the space in the small pages to the official discussions and decisions that filled his day. Structurally these entries resemble a war diary, and occasionally they are even more condensed in sequences without transitions and sentences without verbs. The following is a sample:

June 9, 1942—In the morning at the Community. Last night more than 10 people died; smugglers, etc. Also a movie director Szaro and his father-in-law Goldman. I went to see Auerswald. I submitted a petition for an extension of the curfew hour until 10 o'clock and an application of the Provisioning Authority for food purchases on the

20. War Diary, Armament Command Radom, Group Z, May 5, 1944, once located in Federal Records Center, Alexandria, Va., under original document number Wi/ID 1.4.

free market. I requested the release of the minors from prison, because of overcrowding (1,650 detainees, capacity 500). Recently a transport of Gypsies arrived from Lowicz; they are demoralizing the prison.

I visited an anti-typhus exhibit organized by the Health Department.[21]

The "Community" represents the offices of the council. "Szaro" was Henryk Szapiro. Auerswald was the German ghetto commissar. The Provisioning Authority was the organization of the council concerned with food distribution. The application was a failed effort to obtain permission for food purchases with ghetto funds outside the ghetto in Polish Warsaw, in order to augment official rations. For the Gypsies transported to the ghetto, the prison was the first stop.

When German documents were circulated, a regimen of regulations and usages entered into operation. Two distinctions were made, one between recipients in a different organization or in the field from those in neighboring offices "in house" (*im Hause*), the other between readers who were expected to act upon the communication in some way and those who would be interested only in the contents (*zur Kenntnis* or *nachrichtlich*). The number and variety of addressees in a distribution list (*Verteiler*) indicate only the initial spread of information. Copies could be made by recipients for subordinate officials or commands, to say nothing of oral repetition.

The circulation of the consolidated Einsatzgruppen reports began with twenty-three copies (several of them kept in reserve by the Reich Security Main Office) in July 1941, and escalated to seventy-five copies by April 1942.[22] Such quantities could be produced even when the document was not in a

---

21. Hilberg, *et al.*, *Warsaw Diary of Adam Czerniakow*, p. 364.
22. See Report No. 2, July 2, 1941, Nuremberg trials document NO-4494, and Report No. 193, April 17, 1942, NO-3281.

series. The Regierungspräsident in Łódź, Friedrich Uebel-hoer, proposed on December 10, 1939, the establishment of a ghetto, and that item had a Verteiler of fifty-five copies.[23]

Many communications pertaining to Jewish matters were given security classifications, ranging from *Geheime Reichssache* (Secret State Material) down to *Geheim* (Secret), *Vertraulich* (Confidential), and *Nur für den Dienstgebrauch* (Restricted). The Einsatzgruppen reports were Geheime Reichssache. The ghetto idea of Uebelhoer was marked "*Streng Vertraulich*" (Strictly Confidential) in typed lettering and stamped "Geheim." On the other hand, a railroad official in the Generaldirektion der Ostbahn in Kraków, where schedules were processed for about a thousand trains carrying Jews to their death, testified after the war that the correspondence he saw was designated no more than "Nur für den Dienstgebrauch."[24] A great many of the extant railway items bear no security marking at all. This lack of a classification signifies not only a routine but the sort of business in which Jews were not distinguished from any other group transport, such as Russian workers sent to Germany for labor, or Hitler youths on their way for a summer vacation.

Closely associated with security designations, or their absence, was the mode of transmitting a document. The most sensitive communications were carried by messengers, in the case of high-level military affairs by officers. The common mechanical means were telephonic (*Fernspruch* if noted on paper), teletype (*Fernschreiber*), telegraphic (*Telegramm*), and

---

23. The document is in the United States Holocaust Memorial Museum Archives, Record Group 48.004 (Prague Military Historical Archives), Roll 3.

24. Testimony by Erich Richter, June 11, 1969, Case Albert Ganzenmüller, Landgericht Düsseldorf, 8 Js 430/67, xix, 5–12. Richter handled timetables.

radio (*Funkspruch*). Railroad timetable orders for specific Jewish transports were sent by *Bahndiensttelegramm* (Railroad Service Telegram). Reports by Order Police battalions of shooting operations in the marshes during the summer of 1941 were radioed. British intelligence intercepted these reports, and on September 13, 1941, the chief of the Order Police, Kurt Daluege, admonished the field units not to use radio for messages that, as "Geheime Reichssache," required special precautions, notably "numerical compilations of executions" (*zahlenmässige Angaben über Exekutionen*). Such "proceedings" (*Vorgänge*) were to be transmitted by courier. Daluege's order, itself a Funkspruch, was also intercepted.[25]

Many times, when a document was received, it would be stamped with a date. On occasion the official addressed in the correspondence affixed his handwritten initials at the top of a page without a spelled-out name. Now and then an attentive reader would add a short comment, question mark, exclamation mark, or underlining. In the Administrative Code of 1926, a color scheme was specified for such initialing and notations: a green pencil for a minister, red for a Staatssekretär, blue for a Ministerialdirektor. Outside a ministry, agencies and offices in the field could extend and vary this key. Adolf Eichmann, the specialist for Jewish affairs in the Reich Security Main Office, recalled the following colors for officials in descending order of rank: green for Himmler, blue for Heydrich, orange for Müller, and violet for Eichmann.[26] In the railroad directorate at Minsk, the director used green. Later-

25. See F. H. Hinsley, *British Intelligence in the Second World War* (New York, 1981), II, 669–673, and Richard Breitman, *Official Secrets* (New York, 1998), pp. 54–68. The text of Daluege's order is in Prague Military Historical Archives, Collection SS Pol. Regt. A-3-1-7/4, K. 1. See also a report by Police Regiment Center, November 1, 1941, marked *"Verschlossen"* (closed) in ink, *ibid.*, SS Pol. Regt. A-6-5-6, K. 5.

26. Eichmann, *Ich*, p. 149.

ally his division chiefs were assigned black, red, brown, blue, and violet.[27]

In field offices, records with drastic as well as innocuous contents were not necessarily guarded with care. The official who handled timetables for Jewish transports in the Generaldirektion der Ostbahn noted in postwar testimony that documents lay around openly on the premises.[28] Laxity could befall even the offices of the SS Central Construction Directorate at Auschwitz-Birkenau. On May 5, 1943, the man in charge of that organization, Karl Bischoff, issued an internal order (*Hausverfügung*) in which he pointed to the need for secrecy with special reference to blueprints of the buildings that housed gas chambers and crematories. It was a "matter of course [*selbstverständlich*]," he wrote, that all original drawings were to be kept under lock and key (*unter Verschluss*) by the director of the planning office. That officer, Walter Dejaco, was to be personally responsible for security.[29]

The afterlife of a document was significantly affected by the number of copies that had been made and their routing to various offices. The more extensive the distribution, the greater was the chance that the text survived in at least one location, untouched by bombing or shelling, and abandoned in the course of a retreat or surrender. A prime illustration is the postwar emergence of the consolidated Einsatzgruppen reports. Notwithstanding their top secret classification as

27. Directive of the Direktion, August 11, 1942, United States Holocaust Memorial Museum Archives, Record Group 53.002 (Belarus Central Archives), Roll 1, Fond 378, Opis 1, Folder 267.

28. Testimony by Walter Stier, May 16, 1963, Case Franz Novak, Landgericht Vienna 1416/16, xvi, 355ff.

29. Order by Bischoff, May 5, 1943, United States Holocaust Memorial Museum Archives, Record Group 11.001 (Center for Preservation of Documentary Historical Collections, Moscow), Roll 21, Fond 502, Opis 1, Folder 39. In 1945 these drawings fell into the hands of the Red Army.

Geheime Reichssache by the Security Police, the reassembled set is almost complete.[30] Often the only remaining copy of a communication would be discovered in the records of a receiving agency. A collection captured intact might contain such incoming correspondence from more than one sender. The files of the railway directorate in Minsk, for instance, include a sequence of orders by the 70th Infantry Division with numerous references to the shooting of Jews and Gypsies in Byelorussia. The railways, always interested in sabotage, received these military items for their information.[31]

The composition of postwar statements is different from that of documents. Headings appear only in printed forms that were to be filled out. Pretrial interrogations, court testimony, and interviews have a question-and-answer format, but if a nonlegal conversation was conducted forty or fifty years after the war, the ignorance or deference of a young questioner could allow the respondent to dominate the interchange. Some of these answers, which approach monologues, are renditions conceived entirely by the informant, and they can be lengthy. On the other hand, unpublished statements tendered by witnesses are relatively concise, rarely exceeding ten thousand words. The organizing principle in such submitted accounts is almost always chronology, which is the simplest structure even when precise dates are missing: then, and then, and then.

Zygfryd Halbreich spent sixty-six months, covering almost the entire European war, as an inmate in camps, including

30. Krausnick and Wilhelm, *Die Truppe des Weltanschauungskrieges*, pp. 649–654. The original sequence consisted of 195 reports.

31. See United States Holocaust Memorial Museum Archives, Record Group 53.002 (Belarus Central Archives), Roll 2, Fond 378, Opis 1, Folder 698. Usually receiving agencies filed incoming items in reverse chronological order.

twenty-seven months in Auschwitz. His statement of October 19, 1973, which fills forty typewritten pages, is in the Auschwitz archives. It is evidently a distillation of earlier depositions in several trials. Relatively little deals with his persona. There is a short preamble with his date and place of birth on November 13, 1909, in Bielsko Biała, which belonged to Austria-Hungary when he was born and to Poland after World War I. He notes his training as a pharmacist and his fluency in several languages. But there is no prehistory and only a notation of his 1973 address in Beverly Hills, California. Sectioned into from–to periods, the statement contains his observations of conditions, incidents, and people. Also stated is what he could not recall. In passing he mentions a sister who smuggled explosives to the Jewish inmates working in one of the buildings that housed gassing and cremation facilities, so that they could blow it up. He promises to furnish the Auschwitz archives with her address, so that she might describe her role personally. Once, in the Nordhausen camp, he was assigned to a group of ill persons destined for death. At that moment, in 1945, he was "resigned" to his fate, but while he "accepted the fact" of his selection, he formulated in his thoughts a plan for action. "I intended to save myself," he says, "by jumping out of a train car during my journey." It did not come to that, because Allied bombers hit the railway line.[32]

Halbreich was not a typical victim and his statement, replete with facts laid out one after the other, is not typical of survivor testimony. And yet this lucid, matter-of-fact summation is not comprehensive. He already knew what a prosecutor would seek out and tailored much of what he said to fit the mold of a legal deposition. At the same time he was conscious of those elements of Auschwitz history that only a few sur-

32. Statement by Zygfryd Halbreich, October 19, 1973. Courtesy of Mr. Halbreich.

vivors or he alone might be able to furnish, and he selected his recollections accordingly for the archives of the camp.

Book-length memoirs generally have a more complex structure. Problems of balance, coherence, contrast, and emphasis all come into play. Some authors, including the widely read Auschwitz survivors Rudolf Vrba and Filip Müller, managed this task with literary collaborators.[33] Elie Wiesel, also an Auschwitz survivor, wrote an account that underwent metamorphoses twice under the influence of editors. The original manuscript, in Yiddish, was 862 (presumably handwritten) pages long and not quite finished when Wiesel handed it to an Argentinian publisher. The Yiddish book had 245 pages.[34] The English-language version, translated from the French and given the title *Night*, contains 116 printed pages—about 35,000 words. Everything in the contraction is short: chapters, paragraphs, and sentences.[35]

If an author attempted to write a complete account, either in a single text or a body of works, a discernible division into a before, during, and after would emerge, with the center of gravity in the middle. Wiesel's memoirs of the 1990s, combined with *Night*, constitute such a description. The three components in his case are a quasi-idyllic childhood, the catastrophic darkness of Auschwitz, and recuperation. Not every survivor had a wonderful life before Adolf Hitler's rule, and scarcely anyone's childhood, even in a privileged home, is perfect, but in the memoirs it was always essential to distinguish starkly between the prewar phase and the critical wartime period, lest a reader be misled into concluding that the survivor

33. Vrba and Bestic, *I Cannot Forgive*; and Müller and Freitag, *Sonderbehandlung*.

34. See Elie Wiesel, *Memoirs—All Rivers Run to the Sea* (New York, 1995), pp. 241, 319.

35. See Wiesel's *Night*.

had merely exchanged one misery for another. On the other hand, the liberation and all the good fortunes that one might have had thereafter do not require bright colors. To the contrary, the shadow of the night never disappears. The triumph is muted by the lost years, the victims who died, the mother tongue abandoned in migration, the earliest dreams unrealized. Wiesel became a Nobel laureate, a public idol, a man who met presidents, but in the memoir published at the end of the century he devotes pages to the depression afflicting intellectual survivors. Wiesel is Job, from whom much was taken and to whom very much was given, but who does not forget that many, many lost everything, including their lives.

From a structural view, the memoir written by the Auschwitz commander, Rudolf Höss, in a Polish prison before he was hanged, is a mirror image of a survivor's compartmentalization. In the life of Höss as well, there is a prior existence followed by the Nazi time and a consequence, but the meaning of these periods is the opposite of the survivor experience. Höss describes his childhood as the continual imposition of a father who wanted him to become a priest. Whereas the child Wiesel prayed fervently, Höss felt liberated from religion when his father died. A World War I volunteer and right-wing adherent of the Nazi cause, Höss found fulfillment in the SS, with a family, rank, and responsibility. With the German defeat came the denouement. Höss was arrested, and, he says, the "world" demanded his execution.[36]

For survivors of camps, their experience in this confinement was not only a critical time but one which they divide into two crucial phases: initial shock and subsequent adaptation. Auschwitz survivors often speak of their disbelief when they first encountered the presence of the gas chambers. They go on to detail the physical blows, with fists and truncheons,

36. Rudolf Höss, *Kommandant in Auschwitz* (Stuttgart, 1963).

that they suffered at the hands of strangers, at times without apparent cause. They discuss their discovery of survival strategies and remember moments when some other inmate, whom they might hardly have known, showed them an unexpected kindness or gave them lifesaving help. Some discuss faith. Wiesel, preoccupied with God, asked where He was. Primo Levi, the atheist, resisted the temptation to pray during a selection of the weak for the gas chamber. Prayer at such a moment, he says, would have been "blasphemy." He quotes one inmate who told him that he had always placed his faith in "Joseph." Mystified, Levi had to think for a moment before he realized that the man meant Joseph Stalin.[37]

Endurance was the principal requisite for survival in a camp. The inmate was confronted by crushing conditions, and the struggle for life, waged every day, was prolonged. To carry and cement such a story, a few survivors employ distinctive recurring themes. Primo Levi's references are to language. Levi, Italian born, was particularly conscious of the linguistic isolation of his fellow Italian inmates who, like the Greek Jews, spoke no Yiddish, and who at their peril did not understand warnings or commands. For Levi, Auschwitz was a "Tower of Babel." But diversity is not the only problem when the listener is unable to grasp the meaning of those words that *are* accessible. Once, a Polish Jew tried to convey to Levi how quickly people died in the camp. Levi, who knew some German, was perplexed, and the Yiddish-speaking inmate said, *"Er will nix verstayn"*—he does not want to understand anything. Finally Levi, in the role of witness, speaks of his own attempt, language failing, to explain Auschwitz to the public at large.[38]

A different refrain is found in Wiesel's *Night*. Unlike Levi,

37. Primo Levi, *The Drowned and the Saved* (New York, 1988), pp. 145–147.

38. Primo Levi, *Survival in Auschwitz* (New York, 1961), pp. 27, 47, 62, 66, 95, 103, 113, 151.

Wiesel was only in his teens when he spent months in the same barracks with his father. This relationship becomes a leitmotiv in his account. The father is clearly a burden. "How he had changed! His eyes had grown dim." When his father was beaten by another inmate, Elie did not move. Later when his father, struck again, was crouching and breaking in two "like a dry tree struck by lightning," Elie watched and wanted to run away. Toward the end, "the father had become the child, weak, timid, vulnerable." He was "dead weight," though his son was ashamed of the thought.[39]

It was not only his own reaction to his own father that Wiesel describes. There are three other sons and *their* fathers. One of the fathers was beaten by his thirteen-year-old boy for not making up the bunk properly. Another father was assaulted by his grown son for a bit of bread. The third incident involved a run. The father, a rabbi, had fallen behind and thought that his son had not noticed. Afterward the father was looking for his son and asked Wiesel whether he had seen him. "No," Wiesel answered, but he had momentarily forgotten that the son had seen the father "losing ground, limping, staggering," and had run ahead, not slowing.[40]

Wiesel's *Night* is filled with dialogue, and to some critics this is novelization.[41] Without question it would be hard to recall word for word a conversation or even a remark taking up more than a line. Yet there are narratives with reconstructions much more elaborate than Wiesel's compressed account. A story by one woman, written more than five decades after the war, contains dialogue with long complete sentences following

39. Wiesel, *Night*, pp. 47, 49–50, 65, 117, 118. I am grateful to Leo Pfefferkorn who first called this theme to my attention.

40. *Ibid.*, pp. 75, 113, 102–104.

41. Daniel R. Schwarz, *Imagining the Holocaust* (New York, 1999), pp. 49–73.

one another in substantial paragraphs, and within these quotations the speakers quote various people verbatim.[42] Another author interpolates italicized "recollections" in her text. These inserts, written in the present tense like a diary, are designed to replicate the thoughts she had had at the time.[43] Such tools are sometimes employed in order to reach a readership far removed from an experience that the author is eager to convey. The researcher, however, strives to recapture the past in its pristine state. Incrustation does not open windows to this reality.

42. Lucille Eichengreen with Rebecca Cambi Fromer, *Rumkowski and the Orphans of Łódź* (San Francisco, 2000). Fromer is identified as a teacher, poet, and playwright.

43. Sonia Gaines, *Escape into Darkness* (New York, 1991).

THREE

Style

In the preceding chapter the emphasis was placed on structural elements of the sources, to show how documents and statements were put together. The next step is a closer look inside the written items to identify characteristic modes of expression. This chapter will therefore be focused on style.

Wording is not a random choice. Overall it incorporates the prevailing language of the day and reflects the subculture of the society or organization to which the author belongs. To the extent that typical writing may have additional features, they stem almost invariably from particular settings or objectives. That is notably the case when the subject is laden with psychological strains.

The many devices employed in the materials may be considered under four broad headings. The first points to the use of prosaic formulations. The second highlights special words. The third comprises unvarnished bluntness and its opposite, roundabout language. The fourth deals with various enhancements and refinements.

PROSAIC FORMULATIONS

The overwhelming majority of all communications lacks a marked crescendo. When a researcher first examines documentary files, this flatness is the most striking quality. Most documents are administrative instruments, and they are fashioned in a ready-made style that is either mandatory or the product of long-ingrained habit. At the same time, however, bureaucratic matter-of-factness lends itself to the leveling of sharp-edged subject matter. That effect is visible when accounts of drastic actions are summarized in lists. It is also discernible when the writer introduces such a subject in terms of a problem and its solution.

A sampling of a listing is contained in the report of an Order Police company stationed in the Galician district of the Generalgouvernement. In that region Order Police units, which in peacetime had patrolled the streets of Germany, were deployed with small arms, performing new and very different duties. One of their principal assignments was the roundup of ghetto inhabitants for transport to the death camp of Bełżec. Patrols were also sent out to search for Jewish escapees and others. Company 1 of the Reserve Motorized Police Battalion 133 reported some of the results of a week's activities in the following manner:

Security District North   Rawa Ruska, 1 Aug. 1942
Reserve Police Battalion (mot.) 133   Warsaw Street 17
1st Company   Polish Trade School
    Tel. 136

1. Eliminated [*Beseitigt*] during the period between 25.7 and 1.8.42.
   a) Bandits
   b) Accomplices   9 (including 5 Jews)

c) Beggars 27
d) Thieves 7
e) Vagrants 13
f) Prohibited possession of weapons 1
g) Mentally ill 2
h) Gypsies 24
i) Jews 64

Total 147

"Bandits" in this list were partisans, and "accomplices" their helpers (*Helfershelfer*). Point 1 went on to list arrests, and in point 5, which was the longest paragraph in this one-and-a-half-page report, the commander expressed his concerns about an unguarded depot of captured weapons.[1]

Tabulations may be found in a variety of files. The listing of trains on pages 76 and 77 is from a regional railway office known as the *Generalbetriebsleitung Ost*, abbreviated *GBL Ost*. There were three Generalbetriebsleitungen, and the one in Berlin handled the timetables of trains moving to the east, including those of special trains, or *Sonderzüge*, abbreviated *SdZ*. These trains required special schedules, used only for one trip, as opposed to the posted regular schedules for trains used by the ordinary public. The illustrated table, dated January 16, 1943, is an excerpt for departure listings beginning January 20. It is a "circulatory plan" (*Umlaufplan*) indicating the reuse of cars for several trips within a time frame. The cars belonged to local *Reichsbahndirektionen*, abbreviated *RBD*, in this case Poznań (Posen, abbreviated Psn), Oppeln (Op), and Dresden (Dre). A fourth originator of the rolling stock was the *Generaldirektion der Ostbahn* (Gedob), which covered the five dis-

1. Report of 1st Company (signed Captain Lederer), August 1, 1942, United States Holocaust Memorial Museum Archives, Record Group 11.001 (Center for the Preservation of Historical Documentary Collections, Moscow), Roll 82, Fond 1323, Opis 2, Folder 292b.

tricts of the Generalgouvernement and which was located in Kraków. In column 1 the circulation number (Uml Nr) is given for a bloc of trains provided by one of the Direktionen. The train numbers in column 4 reveal who was transported: ethnic Germans (*Volksdeutsche*, abbreviated Vd), Romanians (Rm), Poles (Po), Polish Jews (Pj), and Western Jews (Da). An emptied train was designated Lp. In columns 5 and 6, abbreviations appear for Auschwitz (Au) and Theresienstadt (Th). Column 7 shows the number of people loaded on a train. All were called "travelers" (*Reisende*). The Umlaufplan was prepared in the GBL Ost/PW, which means the office for *Personenwagen*, or passenger cars, but the figure of 2,000, which applies to Jewish transports departing from Polish cities and the Theresienstadt ghetto, signifies that freight cars were to be used. All the Jews were scheduled to go to death camps, about 18,000 to Auschwitz and 12,000 to Treblinka.[2]

The codes in the railroad plan are essentially abbreviations that were customary in general correspondence about trains. The word "travelers" has its basis in the fact that office PW handled all kinds of trains carrying people, whether they were vacationers or deportees on their last trip. In this document, form and style are therefore indistinguishable. The format *became* the style, and this merger, which was administratively functional, was left undisturbed. It conveys, at first sight, a normal procedure, without any sign to the uninitiated of what was actually happening.

An army captain in charge of a military government post (*Ortskommandantur*) in the Black Sea city of Mariupol could

2. Generalbetriebsleitung Ost/PW (signed Jacobi) to various railroad offices, January 16, 1943, enclosing a compilation and circulatory plan. Only the plan is reproduced here. Pj 111 has no figure in the plan. One of the recipients of the extant copy in Minsk noted, "We are not involved." United States Holocaust Memorial Museum Archives, Record Group 53.002 (Belarus Central Archives) Roll 2, Fond 378, Opis 1, Folder 784. Dr. Karl Jacobi headed PW.

- 5 -

GBL Ost Berlin
PW 113 Bfsv
vom 16.1.1943

12

U m l a u f p l a n
für
die mehrfach zu verwendenden Wagenzüge
zur Bedienung der Sdz für Vd, Rm, Po, Pj u Da.-Umsiedler
in der Zeit vom 20.1. - 18.2.1943

1	2	3	4	5	6	7
Uml Nr	Wagenzug der RBD	am	bedient Zug-Nr	von	nach	Zahl der Reisenden
106	Psn 1 B 15 C	20/21.1.	Vd 201	Kalisch 8.22	Ottersweier	700
		22/23.1.	Lp 202	Ottersweier	Andrzejow	
		25/26.1.	Vd 203	Andrzejow	Linz	500
		27/28.1.	Lp 204	Linz	Kalisch	
		30/31.1.	Vd 205	Kalisch 8.22	Ottersweier	700
107	Op 1 BC 15 C 15 G	25/26.1.	Rm 1	Gleiwitz	Czernowitz	600
		28/29.1.	Lp 2	Czernowitz	Gleiwitz	
		1/2.2.	Rm 3	Gleiwitz	Czernowitz	600
		4/5.2.	Lp 4	Czernowitz	Ratibor	
		8/9.2.	Rm 5	Ratibor	Czernowitz	600
		11/12.2.	Lp 6	Czernowitz	Gleiwitz	
		15/16.2.	Rm 7	Gleiwitz	Czernowitz	600
		18/19.2.	Lp 8	Czernowitz	Gleiwitz	
121	Psn 21 C	5/6.2.	Pj 107	Bialystok 9.00	Auschwitz 7.57	2000
		7/8.2.	Lp 108	Auschwitz	Bialystok	
		9.2.	Pj 127	Bialystok 9.00	Treblinka 12.10	2000
		9.2.	Lp 128	Treblinka 21.18	Bialystok 1.30	
		11.2.	Pj 131	Bialystok 9.00	Treblinka 12.10	2000
		11.2.	Lp 132	Treblinka 21.18	Bialystok 1.30	
		13.2.	Pj 135	Bialystok 9.00	Treblinka 12.10	2000
		13.2.	Lp 136	Treblinka 21.18	Bialystok 1.30	

A train schedule, dated January 16, 1943, showing departure listings
beginning January 20.

L ⌄ ?

- 6 -

1	2	3	^	5	6	7
122	Psn 21 C	6/7.2.	Pj 109	Bialystok 9.00	Auschwitz 12.10	2000
		8/9.2.	Lp 110	Auschwitz	Bialystok	
		10.2.	Pj 129	Bialystok 9.00	Treblinka 12.10	2000
		10.2.	Lp 130	Treblinka 21.18	Bialystok 1.30	
		12.2.	Pj 133	Bialystok 9.00	Treblinka 12.10	2000
		12.2.	Lp 134	Treblinka 21.18	Grodno	
		14.2.	Pj 163	Grodno 5.40	Treblinka 12.10	2000
		14.2.	Lp 164	Treblinka	Scharfenwiese	
123	Psn 21 C	7/8.2.	Pj 111	Bialystok	Auschwitz	
		8.2.	Lp 112	Auschwitz	Myslowitz	
126	Gedob 1 BC 16 C	25/26.1.	Po 61	Bamocz 8.20	Berlin Whgen 17.30	1000
		29/30.1.	Da 13	Barlin Mob 17.20	Auschwitz 10.48	1000
		31.1/1.2.	Lp 14	Auschwitz	Zamocz	
		3/4.2.	Po 65	Zamocz	Auschwitz	1000
		4.2.	Lp 66	Auschwitz	Myslowitz	
127	Gedob 1 BC 16 C	29/30.1.	Po 63	Zamocz 8.20	Berlin Whgen 17.30	1000
		2/3.2.	Da 15	Berlin Mob 17.20	Auschwitz 10.48	1000
		4/5.2.	Lp 16	Auschwitz	Litzmannstadt	
128	Dre 21 C 1 G	20/21.1.	Da 101	Theresienst.	Auschwitz	2000
		21/22.1.	Lp 102	Auschwitz	Theresienstadt	
		23/24.1.	Da 103	Th	Au	2000
		24/25.1.	Lp 104	Au	Th	
		26/27.1.	Da 105	Th	Au	2000
		27/28.1.	Lp 106	Au	Th	
		29/30.1.	Da 107	Th	Au	2000
		30/31.1.	Lp 108	Au	Th	
		1/2.2.	Da 109	Th	Au	2000
		2.2.	Lp 110	Auschwitz	Myslowitz	

not avail himself of preset tables and enumerations. He had to write more, but he did so under five captions that, with some variations, served all the Ortskommandanturen in the region:

I. Military
II. Political
III. Administrative
IV. Economic
V. General

Filling three single-spaced pages, he described his own experiences in a somewhat expansive manner and recapitulated more sparsely what he had been told. In the first section he went into detail about his arrival in the city at 6 p.m. on October 20, 1941, after a twelve-hour ride on almost impassable roads. The next section, with recognizable traces of cataloging, begins as follows:

II. Political
Mariupol has approximately 250,000 inhabitants, of whom 80% are Russians, 10% Ukrainians, 8% Jews, and approximately 600 ethnic Germans.
8,000 Jews were executed by the SD.
The vacated Jewish apartments were taken over by the Ortskommandantur. The Jewish clothes, underwear, etc., were collected by the Ortskommandantur and after cleaning distributed to the field hospital, prisoner-of-war camp, and ethnic Germans.
The civilian population is not hostile to the German troops. Looting took place during the first few days like everywhere.
The Kommandantur began as its main task the identification of the ethnic Germans. . . .[3]

3. Ortskommandantur I/853 in Mariupol to *Oberfeldkommandantur* 553/Qu (Quartermaster), October 29, 1941, National Archives, Record

The sentence about the killing of the Jews is the shortest in the passage, and the author achieved maximum brevity by contracting "Security Police and Security Service" (*Sicherheitspolizei und Sicherheitsdienst*) to the customary "SD," without identifying the shooters as an element of Einsatzgruppe D. As read today, the single line stands out and arrests attention. Yet at the time it fit into the author's logical division of thought. He begins with the city's prewar population, subtracts the Jews, describes the remaining inhabitants who are quiescent except for some looting, and goes on to the local ethnic Germans who are his stated main concern.

The following two items are rare examples of the laconic mode. As single-sentence documents, they obviously do not constitute a list, but they do suggest a routine of sufficiency in writing receipts. The first, from Auschwitz, is dated December 1, 1942:

> Confirmation of Transfer [*Übergabebestätigung*]
> The Transfer of—532—Jews from Norway is hereby confirmed.
>
> The Camp Commander
I. A. Stark
Sergeant
SS ~~2nd Lieutenant~~[4]

Almost at the same time, an ordinary Jewish policeman (*Ordner*) wrote this note on November 19, 1942, in Będzin, Upper Silesia:

Group 242, T 501, Roll 56. Note also the report by the same officer from the Crimean city of Simferopol on November 14, 1941, where the killing of eleven thousand Jews is recounted in a virtually identical manner. *Ibid.* The signature of the officer is illegible in both documents.

4. Confirmation, Auschwitz/Kommandantur II, December 1, 1942, facsimile in Oskar Mendelsohn, *Jødenes Historie i Norge* (Oslo, 1983), II, 130. The signature and rank above the crossed-out line are handwritten.

To the Order Service Group in Warthenau [Zawiercie]
We acknowledge the receipt of 10 persons
Leopold Izrael Schneider
Order Service Man 118, Sosnowiec[5]

The idea of problem solving is a common thread in the files of the bureaucracy. As a matter of course, the Jews were always considered a "problem," and the measures against them were, in the same vein, "solutions." The following two excerpts from military reports illustrate this frame of reference.

The first is a recapitulation of events in the area of the 454th Security Division from August 16 to September 15, 1941, by the chief of its Section VII (Military Government), *Oberkriegsverwaltungsrat* von Winterfeld. The division was located in the Ukrainian city of Zhitomir and points north. When units of the SS and Police swept through this region, they began by killing Jewish men. By August they had added a significant number of Jewish women to their targeted victims. And that left Jewish children. In a short paragraph Winterfeld states:

> One can hardly talk about the Jewish question anymore. In a few localities the care of orphaned Jewish children and infants caused temporary difficulties; in the meantime, however, the SD redressed this situation.[6]

---

5. Handwritten receipt, United States Holocaust Memorial Museum Archives, Record Group 15.060 (Żydowski Instytut Historyczny), Roll 2, Sygn. 212/14 (Transit Camp Sosnowiec).

6. Situation report of 454th Security Division/VII, signed Oberkriegsverwaltungsrat von Winterfeld, September 23, 1941, German Federal Archives R 94/26.

A few months later, *Kriegsverwaltungsrat* Heine of the
Feldkommandantur 197 noted:

> Insofar as still at hand, continual actions against Jews are
> carried out by the GFP. Any other measures (food and
> labor allocation) are, therefore, unnecessary.[7]

The GFP (*Geheime Feldpolizei*) refers to the army's own intelligence sections.

Sometimes problems arose in the course of carrying out a
"solution." In the Byelorussian capital of Minsk, a ghetto had
been created for local Jews. At the end of 1941 and again in
1942, large numbers of Jews were transported to Minsk in
slow-moving trains, each loaded with one thousand deportees,
from Vienna, Theresienstadt, and various points in Germany.
By the spring and summer of 1942, the deportees were shot
immediately, without stopping in the ghetto, by a detachment
of Security Police that was stationed there. The police needed
some respite from the strain of so much shooting, and they
tried to free the weekends by negotiating the arrival times
with officials of the Railway Directorate Center in Minsk.
The agreed stipulations were recorded in a memorandum by
the Security Police on May 23, 1942.

> In connection with today's meeting of *Reichsbahnoberrat*
> Reichardt and *Reichsbahnräte* Logemann and Kayser with
> SS 1st Lieutenant [*Obersturmführer*] Lütkenhus, I am sum-
> marizing the result of the negotiations briefly as follows:
>
> 1. The transport awaited here before Whitmonday will
> be delayed in Koydanov so that it will not pull in until the
> night from Monday to Tuesday.

7. Report by Kriegsverwaltungsrat Heine of Feldkommandantur 197
for November 15, 1941, to December 15, 1941, dated December 15, 1941,
National Archives, Record Group 242, T 501, Roll 34.

2. The Railway Directorate Center will request the appropriate railway office to move the departure time of future transports accordingly.

3. Pending the approval of this change in the time table, the Railway Directorate is prepared on its part to shunt all future transports to a siding in Koydanov in such a way that the train will pull in from Sunday to Monday, or some other day with the exception of Friday, Saturday, and Sunday.

4. So far as possible the Railway Directorate will direct transports arriving in Minsk to a track that will enable the trucks I am dispatching to drive up close.

My special thanks for the accommodation in this matter.

[Written Signature] Dr. Georg Heuser[8]

At the time of the deportations, the Jewish community organizations in various cities of Europe had an acute problem. They were directed by the Security Police to carry out several essential functions in the preparatory work for the deportations, from the keeping of accurate addresses to the notification, concentration, guarding, and care of the prospective victims entering the trains. The Jewish functionaries in turn had to convince the victims of the necessity for punctual and meticulous compliance with all instructions. In the fall of 1941, before the Jewish leadership had any inkling of the ultimate fate that would befall the deportees, the tone of its

8. The Kommandeur of Security Police and Security Service White Ruthenia (Byelorussia) IIb to "Reichsbahn Direktorat" (the correct designation at the time would have been Haupteisenbahndirektion) Center, attention Reichsbahnoberrat Reichardt, May 23, 1942, United States Holocaust Memorial Museum Archives, Record Group 53.002 (Belarus Central Archives), Roll 2, Fond 378, Opis 1, Folder 284.

communications to the community was designed to instill self-confidence. When, for example, the Jewish consistory in Luxembourg had to notify its members on October 5, 1941, that all of them would soon have to leave, and that their destination would be in the east, the phrase "heads high" (*Kopf hoch*) was used twice in the notice.[9] The first train was scheduled to leave at twelve minutes after midnight on October 17, 1941, to the ghetto of Łódź, where it was to arrive at approximately 11 a.m. the next day.[10] A total of 334 were aboard. Eleven came back after the war.[11]

By 1942 the deportations from all areas under direct German control were quickening. Jewish leaders in Berlin were walking a tightrope as they weighed their dual role of assisting the Gestapo in the roundups and helping the shrinking community as much and for as long as possible. In this predicament, the Jewish bureaucrats began to think in terms of reducing the psychological burden placed on the victims by enlisting them in an efficient procedure devoid of incidents, and they phrased the notifications accordingly.

The office of the Berlin community that sent out the notices was the "Housing Advisory Bureau" (*Wohnungsberatungsstelle*), which had the most recent addresses and which worked on the deportation lists. The following communication was received by Mannheim Spicker, whose destination was Theresienstadt in the "Protectorate of Bohemia and Moravia." Spicker did not survive.

9. Consistory of the Jewish Community in Luxembourg to all the Jews in the Grand Duchy, October 25, 1941, United States Holocaust Memorial Museum Archives, Accession No. 1997. A. 008 (Grand Duchy Archives, Collection Chef der Zivilverwaltung, Luxemburg), Roll 2.

10. Consistory to Luxembourg Jews, October 7, 1941, *ibid.*

11. Paul Cerf, *Longtemps j'aurai mémoire* (Luxembourg, 1974), pp. 198–204.

Jewish Community Berlin [stamped] July 3, 1942

Mr./Mrs./Miss Mannheim Isr. [Israel] Spicker
Boxhagen Street 120
Transport No. 0 2019
Re: Migration [*Abwanderung*]

Your migration to the Protectorate was officially ordered for Monday, July 13, 1942. This order applies to
you, your wife, and your unmarried relatives, if they were
called upon to hand in the property declaration.

On Wednesday, July 8, 1942, between 9 a.m. and 1
p.m., your luggage is to be delivered to the clothes depot at
the underlined district office

I. Center	August St. 17
II. South	Thielsch Shore 10/16
III. North	Eberswalder St. 26
IV. Southwest	Münchener St. 37
V. Charlottenburg	Pestalozzi St. 14/15

[The following paragraph is indented and marked with
heavy vertical lines in the left margin.]

It is not possible to take along the luggage when
you are escorted from your apartment. You may
take with you, while escorted away, only hand luggage that you can carry yourself and is small in
weight and size. This includes absolutely: night
items, blanket, plate, spoon, cup, and food.

On Thursday, July 19, 1942, at 8 a.m., your apartment
will be sealed by an official. You must be ready at that moment. Apartment and room keys are to be handed to the
official. You yourself will then be brought in a car sent by us
to the collecting shelter at Grosse Hamburger Strasse 26.

Any savings account books, etc., securities so far as they
are not kept in a bank, mortgage certificates, bank receipts,
and so forth, in short all papers that indicate something

about your property, and any deposit box key, are to be handed over in a sturdy, unsealed but sealable envelope when you arrive at the collecting center at Grosse Hamburger Strasse 26. Your name, address, and transport number are to be entered exactly on the envelope.

We will provide meals at the collecting point and during the train journey. Food in your household, especially bread slices for the evening, should be brought along in the hand luggage.

At the collecting shelter and during the train journey, persons who treat the ill [*Krankenbehandler*] and nursing personnel will be available. Any necessary drugs will be supplied solely by health personnel. Transmission of any written or oral messages, as well as any tasks requested of helpers at the transit home, is prohibited.

The appended sheet of instructions is to be noted. We ask you sincerely to follow these instructions with precision and to prepare for transport with calm and circumspection.

Our members who are selected for migration must be aware that their personal conduct and orderly fulfillment of all directions can contribute decisively to the smooth processing of the transport. It is to be taken for granted that we will do everything to the extent permitted to stand by our community members and render them every possible help.

The Jewish Community in Berlin
The Directorate[12]

12. Photocopy of the notice, through the courtesy of Ruth-Monika Ribold, granddaughter of Mannheim Spicker. The address of the sender on the envelope is: Jüdische Kultusgemeinde, Wohnungsberatungsstelle, Berlin N 4, Oranienburg St. 31. The office was headed by Martha Mosse. In the notice, the middle name "Israel" was compulsory. No district clothing depot is underlined.

SPECIAL WORDS AND SYMBOLS

Frequently the sources contain words that are not self-explanatory. Even though these nouns, verbs, and adjectives are clearly recognizable, they may not be fully understood because they acquired novel meanings during the Nazi era.[13] These uses evolved in the course of an unfolding development and are rooted in specific phases of that process. Some were mandated as part of official terminology, others were generated to express an attitude.

When a word was endowed with an official definition, its application had direct consequences. There were terms to categorize people and a vocabulary to delineate actions. In both cases the creation of this nomenclature was an elaborate undertaking by upper-level bureaucrats who wrote drafts, comments, instructions, and explanations. The ideological hue of the correspondence is unmistakable, but the reasons for the effort were utilitarian. Precisely set boundaries enabled a subordinate to make more reliable decisions in allocating an individual to the proper group or taking the right measure in the appropriate way.

Perhaps the greatest difficulty was posed by the concept of "Jews" itself. Although Jewry was a target from the beginning, a workable definition was not written for several years. In November 1932, more than two months before Hitler came to power, the Prussian Interior Ministry attempted to limit the permissibility of name changes. The question arose, which approvals were to be denied? One of the topics under discussion was that "of Jewish-sounding names" (*jüdischen oder jüdisch klingenden Namen*). On one draft an official wrote in

13. For a dictionary of several terms discussed in this chapter and others not covered here, see Cornelia Schmitz-Berning, *Vokabular des National-sozialismus* (Berlin, 1998).

December that the issue was the "identification of blood-based connections" (*die Kenntlichmachung der blutmässigen Zusammenhänge*). At that point there was still hesitation to prohibit explicitly the substitution of a "German" name, and the word "German" was crossed out, but on March 25, 1933, after Hitler had become chancellor, the name expert of the ministry, Regierungsrat Hans Globke, wrote: "As a matter of principle, permission will not be granted for a name change that is designed to hide non-Aryan descent."[14] In a published law, the term "non-Aryan" appeared for the first time during the following month. The law, which dealt with dismissals from the civil service, stipulated that a non-Aryan was anyone with at least one Jewish grandparent.[15]

Two years later another law was promulgated, this time to prohibit "Jews" from forming a marriage or having extra-marital relations with persons of "German or related [*artverwandten*] blood."[16] Now the definition of the term "Jew" became urgent. What followed was an elaborate scheme in which a "non-Aryan" was one of the following:

Any person who "is a Jew" [in the original: *Jude ist*]
This category embraced everyone, regardless of religion, if at least three "parts" of the individual's grandparentage (*Grosselternteile*) were Jews by religion. Because that per-

---

14. Correspondence once located in the Zentralarchiv (Central Archives of the German Democratic Republic) Potsdam, Collection 15.01 Reichsministerium des Innern 27 403. Globke's letter was sent to Regierungsrat Kriege in the Justice Ministry.

15. Law for the Restoration of the Professional Civil Service, April 7, 1933, RGBl I, 175.

16. Law for the Protection of German Blood and Honor, September 15, 1935, RGBl I, 1146. Neither "German blood" (*deutschblütig*) nor "related" was defined in the law. See Schmitz-Berning, *Vokabular*, pp. 70–71, 149–150.

son's own religion was irrelevant, the term "racial Jew" (*Rassejude*) came into use.

Any person who "also counts as a Jew" [*Als Jude gilt auch*]
Also classified as Jewish was someone with only two Jewish grandparents, if the individual belonged to the Jewish religion or was married to a Jewish person at the time the law went into effect, but that person was called a *Geltungsjude*.

A *Mischling* of the 1st Degree
A half-Jewish individual who did not belong to the Jewish religion and was not married to a Jewish person when the law went into effect.

A *Mischling* of the 2nd Degree
A quarter Jew by descent, regardless of religion.[17]

Anyone who belonged to the Jewish religion was a *Glaubensjude*. If that individual was a Mischling of the 2nd Degree or even an Aryan, he or she was considered to have joined the Jewish ranks voluntarily, but ordinarily the option of renouncing this choice was left open. At the time of the deportations from the German Reich, the Geltungsjuden, Mischlinge, and those Glaubensjuden of predominantly German descent were spared, although the whereabouts of the Geltungsjuden and Glaubensjuden were tracked alongside the Rassejuden in the records.[18]

Noteworthy is the fact that there were not only Jewish

17. "Jews" were defined in the First Ordinance to the Reich Citizenship Law, November 14, 1935, RGBl I, 1333. Mischlinge were defined in bureaucratic circulars. See Wilhelm Stuckart and Rolf Schiedermair, *Rasse- und Erbpflege in der Gesetzgebung des Reichs*, 5th ed. (Leipzig, 1944), p. 17.

18. See the report of the Gestapo plenipotentiary with the district office of the Reichsvereiningung (Jewish community) in Frankfurt, April 16, 1943, in Kommission der Erforschung der Geschichte der Frankfurter Juden, *Dokumente zur Geschichte der Frankfurter Juden* (Frankfurt, 1966), pp. 488–490.

Mischlinge but also Gypsy Mischlinge (*Zigeuner Mischlinge*). In the breakdown of the Gypsy population, the definitions were, however, markedly different:

Z   Pure indigenous Gypsies (Sinte tribe), or those pure foreign Gypsies (Roma, Lalleri, and other tribes) who were unable to prove German nationality.

Gypsy Mischlinge

ZM+ Predominantly Gypsy "blood shares."

ZM   Equal Gypsy and German blood shares, particularly offspring of two half-Gypsy parents.

ZM 1 Gypsy Mischling of the 1st Degree. Descended from a pure Gypsy and a pure German.

ZM 2 Gypsy Mischling of the 2d Degree. Descended from only one Gypsy grandparent.

ZM- Descended from only one Gypsy great-grand-parent.

An additional designation was reserved for people who were not Gypsies or Gypsy Mischlinge but who roved in a Gypsy-like manner. They were given the lettering NZ (not Gypsy, or *Nicht Zigeuner*).[19]

Gypsies and Gypsy Mischlinge also suffered fates different from those of people labeled Jews and Jewish Mischlinge. Within the Greater German Reich, which included incorporated areas, deportations affected pure Gypsies and Mischlinge from 1940 to 1942. At the beginning of 1943,

19. Circular decree, "Bekämpfung der Zigeunerplage" (Battling the Gypsy Nuisance), December 8, 1938, *Ministerialblatt des Reichs- und Preussischen Ministeriums des Innern*, 1938, p. 2105, and circular decree of August 7, 1941, on "race-biological" expert opinions, *ibid.*, 1941, p. 1442. Classifications were based on investigations of ancestry and personal characteristics conducted by the Rassenhygienischen Forschungsstelle (Race-Hygienic Research Center) of the Health Office of the Interior Ministry.

refinements were introduced. The pure Gypsies of the Sinti and Lalleri tribes as well as "good" Gypsy Mischlinge accepted by the extended family clans of those tribes were generally exempted, whereas pure Gypsies of the Roma tribe, and all other Mischlinge except for those in a mixed marriage or with a fixed domicile and steady employment, were sent to Auschwitz. Moreover, the pure Gypsies and the exempted Mischlinge, except for pure Sinte and "good" Mischlinge, were subject to sterilization. What accounts for this contrast in the treatment of Jews and Gypsies? In the Jewish community the full-Jews greatly outnumbered the Jewish Mischlinge, whereas in the Sinte population the Mischlinge were a 90 percent majority. The Jewish Mischlinge were protected because the German parent was still a valued German. The Gypsy Mischlinge, on the other hand, were regarded as the sons and daughters of the lowest of the low in German society, such as a German mother who might have been illegitimate, or an itinerant German father who was "at best" a musician, actor, or day laborer. Generally, the Gypsy "Mischlinge" were regarded as unreliable, lazy, and unsteady, and intermarriage among these people was believed to perpetuate an inferior group. Because of such thinking, a word like "Mischling" could have divergent meanings, one applicable to Jews, the other to Gypsies.[20]

20. For the rationale of ranking the Gypsy Mischlinge, see R. Ritter, "Die Bestandaufnahme der Zigeuner und Zigeunermischlinge in Deutschland," in *Der öffentliche Gesundheitsdienst*, vol. 6, February 5, 1941, pp. 306–318. The Auschwitz decree was issued in print form on January 29, 1943, by the Criminal Police (Reich Security Main Office) V A 2. Text in Hans-Joachim Döring, *Die Zigeuner im Nationalsozialistischen Staat* (Hamburg, 1964), pp. 214–218. For two major monographs on the treatment of the Gypsies, see Michael Zimmermann, *Rassenutopie und Genozid* (Hamburg, 1996), and Guenter Lewy, *The Nazi Persecution of the Gypsies* (New York, 2000).

Sometimes two words were needed to describe the same status. Germans were allowed the choice of a religious denomination, usually Evangelical Lutheran or Catholic, or else no denomination at all. Those who dispensed with a religious membership could enter "believing in God" (*gottgläubig*) in their personnel records.[21] As the Chief of the Party Chancellery noted at one time: "When we National Socialists use the word 'gottgläubig' we do not refer to the same God as true Christians." To be sure, this explanation caused difficulties in Catholic Spain and was subsequently abandoned,[22] but the expression itself remained in the documents. Among Jews, as well, there were people who—without adopting another religion—wished to disassociate themselves from the Jewish religious community, but these persons were not allowed to use the word "gottgläubig." They had to write "without belief" (*glaubenslos*).[23] In this manner any possible confusion between churchless Germans and unaffiliated Jews was eliminated.

The practice of dual vocabulary was extended also to professions and functions. A German could be a lawyer (*Rechtsanwalt*), a Jew only a "consultant" (*Konsulent*). A German could be a doctor (*Arzt*), but a Jew was allowed only the title "treater of the ill" (Krankenbehandler). For Germans there was a profusion of terms designating the scope of power; the principal Jewish authority, particularly in Poland, was most often the "Council of Elders" (*Ältestenrat*). German police were police;

21. See the letter by Interior Minister Wilhelm Frick, January 3, 1938, in the Diary of Justice Minister Franz Gürtner, January 6, 1938, National Archives, Record Group 238, M 978, Roll 3.

22. Memorandum by Bormann, enclosed by Staatssekretär of the Foreign Office Ernst Bohle to Himmler, October 27, 1942, National Archives, Record Group 242, T 175, Roll 68.

23. Decree by Interior Ministry, June 12, 1941 (Reichsministerialblatt), RBM1 i V, 1053. The decree was issued with the agreement of the Party Chancellery and the Church Ministry.

Jews performing police functions were the "Jewish Order Service" (*Jüdischer Ordnungsdienst*).

Much effort was expended on formulas of descent affecting persons of Jewish or Gypsy background, but no such precision was lavished on definitions of other ethnic groups. The principle employed in deciding who was what in German-controlled territory was most often citizenship, as indicated in prewar records or, in the case of occupied regions in the Soviet Union, the nationality (meaning ethnic group) listed in personal documents issued by Soviet authorities. The identified groups were then placed in a rank order, from the most treasured, who were ethnically German, to the least appreciated, namely the Slavs, who were placed just above the Gypsies and Jews. This differentiation had to be codified in newly coined designations.

The non-Jewish, non-Gypsy population of Germany was treated as a homogeneous nation with the stress on *one* people (*ein Volk*). The law prohibiting mixed marriages and mixed extramarital relations involving Jews did apply to persons of either "German" or "related" blood, but this formula was undoubtedly chosen to blur the question of the precise bloodlines that could be paired with the German. If one pays attention to names, quite a few individuals stand out, even in the upper ranks of various hierarchies, whose ancestry was at least partially French, Dutch, Danish, Italian, Greek, or—judging from "ski" endings in family names—Polish. The consoling thought about these people, born in Germany, was that their forebears had long been "Germanized" (*eingedeutscht*).

"German blood," in turn, was found in many foreign countries. The carriers of this blood were the "ethnic Germans" (*Volksdeutsche*), often identified by their German names, or some comprehension of the German language, or some other indicator of adherence to German culture. Ethnic Germans were encouraged to move to Germany, especially from territories allocated to the Soviet power sphere under the terms of the secret protocol attached to the August 1939 nonaggression pact between Germany and the USSR. The immigrants were eligible for German citizenship, usually on a revocable basis.[24]

In Germany, ethnic Germans were particularly welcomed by the Nazi party, which placed some of them in important positions in its newly formed and growing apparatus.[25] Inside occupied Poland, Yugoslavia, and Soviet territories, ethnic Germans were highly privileged. In conquered regions they were armed and banded together in a *Selbstschutz*. In Slovakia, a satellite state, they had a uniformed *Freiwillige Schutzstaffel*, abbreviated *FS*. In the Romanian-occupied zone between the Dnestr and Bug rivers, known as Transnistria, they had a *Kommando*, nominally under the SS Ethnic German Welfare Service (*Volksdeutsche Mittelstelle*, abbreviated *VOMI*). Both the FS and the VOMI Kommando were engaged in anti-Jewish

24. See the statistics as of December 1942 in Rolf-Dieter Müller, *Hitlers Ostkrieg und die Siedlungspolitik* (Frankfurt am Main, 1991), pp. 200–204.

25. Hitler's deputy in the Nazi party was Rudolf Hess, born in Alexandria, Egypt, and his ideological chief, later Minister of Eastern Occupied Territories, Hans Rosenberg, half-Estonian by descent, was born in Tallin. Walter Darré, the party's chief of farmers who later became Minister of Agriculture, was born in Belgrano, Argentina, and Herbert Backe, who succeeded Darré in the Ministry of Agriculture, was born in Batum, Caucasus, in the Russian Empire. Dr. Leonardo Conti, Reich health chief in the Nazi party and Staatssekretär for Health in the Interior Ministry, was born of an Italian father and a German mother in Lugano, Switzerland. See Hermann Weiss, ed., *Biographisches Lexikon zum Dritten Reich* (Frankfurt am Main, 1998). Reichskommissar of the Netherlands Arthur Seyss-Inquart, Military Commander in Serbia General Franz Böhme, Plenipotentiary General in Croatia Glaise von Horstenau, Gouverneur of Galicia Otto Wächter, and Chief of the Reich Security Main Office (after Heydrich's assassination) Ernst Kaltenbrunner, were Austrians.

activities. In Transnistria the Kommando was shooting Jews en masse.

A concept somewhat wider than "German" was "Germanic" (*germanisch*). In the SS, the Norwegian, Finnish, Swedish, Danish, Dutch, Flemish, and Swiss volunteers were called "Germanic," and when questions arose of who, among the myriads of foreign workers in the Reich, was allowed to have sexual relations with German women, this high privilege was granted to Norwegians, Danes, and the Dutch.[26]

In the periphery of the Germans and Germanic peoples were those of "related blood" (*artverwandtes Blut*), who were mentioned but not defined in the Law for the Protection of German Blood and Honor. At the beginning of 1943, Himmler ruled that this circle comprised the Celtic, Romance, Baltic, and Slavic nations.[27] In the occupied USSR quite a few Balts and Slavs were recruited as collaborators. These indigenous helpers were local inhabitants and eligible prisoners of war. Initially they were not supposed to be soldiers or regular policemen, nor were their units designated as companies or battalions. They were not given regular uniforms or more than a few firearms with limited ammunition, and at first they wore armbands with inscriptions indicating their auxiliary role in the German army.[28] All these men also had to be called something that would deliniate their status above the popula-

26. Himmler to Hitler, January 1943, National Archives, Record Group 242, T 175, Roll 124. Order by Dresden Security Police (signed Zapp), January 2, 1945, Staatsarchiv Leipzig, Polizeipräsident Leipzig V 4000.

27. Circular of Reich Security Main Office/ID, February 23, 1943, United States Holocaust Memorial Museum Archives, Record Group 15.034 (Commander of Security Police, Lublin district), Roll 1.

28. Directive of the High Command of the Army/Gen Qu, August 14, 1941, German Federal Archives, RW 41/4. High Command of the Army to Army Group North, November 25, 1941, National Archives, Record Group 242, T 311, Roll 99.

tion from which they had been lifted but below their German masters. The appropriate set of designations called for linguistic dexterity. As shown in the simplified diagram below, the terminology was neither uniform nor durable.[29]

	Invasion period	Secured areas	Consolidation phase
North	*Selbstschutz* Self-Protection	*Hilfspolizei* -*HIPO* Auxiliary Police	*Hilfspolizei*
Center	*Hilfspolizei*	*Ordnungsdienst* -*OD* Order Service	*Ordnungsdienst*
South	*Selbstschutz*	*Miliz* Militia	*Hilfspolizei*

Several reasons account for this diversity. Only the Baltic area, conquered by Army Group North, and Ukraine, traversed by Army Group South, contained inhabitants who were striving for independence, and there the German invaders could observe or presume sufficient anti-Soviet hostil-

---

29. Order of Commander, Army Group Rear Area 103/Ic (signed by General Karl von Roques), July 2, 1941, German Federal Archives, RH 22/187. Order by 18th Army (north), July 7, 1941, National Archives, Record Group 242, T 315, Roll 574. Order of Army Group Rear Area South July 22, 1941, *ibid.*, T 501, Roll 7. Order of Commander, Rear Army Group Center, July 24, 1941, German Federal Archives, RH 26-102/12. Order of High Command of the Army/Gen Qu, August 18, 1941, *ibid.*, RW 41/4. Order of 454th Security Division (in the south), August 1941, *ibid.*, RH 26-454/47. Order by Commander, Rear Army Group Area Center, October 30, 1941, *ibid.*, RH 22/225. Order by Rear Army Group Area South, National Archives, Record Group 242, T 501, Roll 23.

ity to harness it immediately in the form of "self-protection" units. The term "Selbstschutz," however, lost its meaning once the areas were secure. The only visible features that remained were the national colors on armbands: red-white-red for the Latvian *Heimatschutz* (Homeland Protection),[30] blue-white-black for Estonians,[31] and yellow-blue for Ukrainians.[32] In the center, where the Byelorussians and Russians were encountered, there was only a Hilfspolizei with white armbands. The word "Hilfspolizei," it turned out, had created the "mistaken impression" (*irrtümliche Auffassung*) that this organ had been given the prerogatives of a police force. Hence the new term was "Ordnungsdienst."[33] In the south, the term "Miliz," with its military connotations, was dropped in favor of "Hilfspolizei."[34]

The struggle with words did not end there. The army needed not only police helpers, enlisted locally, but also an auxiliary for guarding bridges and military installations. These men, recruited mainly from prisoner-of-war camps, were called *Hilfswachmannschaften* (HIWA).[35] Later the army re-

30. Order of 11th Infantry Division, July 7, 1941, National Archives, Record Group 242, T 315, Roll 547.
31. Order of 93d Infantry Division, July 30, 1941, *ibid.*, T 315, Roll 1164.
32. Order of 454th Security Division, August 1941, German Federal Archives, RH 26-454/47.
33. Order of Commander of Rear Army Group Area Center (General Max von Schenckendorff), July 24, 1941, *ibid.*, RH 26-102/12. Ordnungsdienst was the designation used for Jewish police in ghettos and labor camps.
34. Order by 454th Security Division, August 1941, *ibid.*, RH 26-26-254/47. Order of Army Group Rear Area South (General Erich Friderici), November 14, 1941, National Archives, Record Group 242, T 501, Roll 23.
35. Order of November 14, 1941, *ibid.* Order by 213th Security Division/Ia, April 9, 1942, German Federal Archives, RH 26-213/9. Indigenous personnel (volunteers from among local residents and prisoners of war) assigned for permanent duty to military units received the designation *Hilfswillige* (HIWIS). They were not supposed to exceed 10 percent of a

sorted to the establishment of an armed force consisting of "Cossacks" and "Turkic" peoples. These units were organized by nationality and were considered "co-combatants with equal rights," standing shoulder to shoulder with German soldiers.[36]

A large group of native helpers, both stationary and mobile, were subordinated to the German Order Police. These men received the designation *Schutzmannschaft* (Schuma).[37] Here too, distinctions were made in the matter of salaries, promotions, and the like, favoring the Baltic contingents, but no attention was called to that separation until much later, when the Balts, no longer *Schutzmänner*, were called only by their nationality.

The Selbstschutz, Miliz, Ordnungsdienst, Hilfspolizei, and Schutzmannschaft performed police functions that included "political" tasks, such as a deployment, either occasionally or more intensively over stated periods of time, for the seizure, guarding, or shooting of Jews. The evolved HIWA was associated mainly with military security and the full-fledged military co-combatants saw battle. By then, of course, much of the killing of the Soviet Jews had already been accomplished.

A special problem arose with respect to the word "partisans," which at first referred to insurgents in Kaunas and other Baltic cities who rose against Soviet rule just before the entry of German troops.[38] Not long after that period, however, Byelorussians and Ukrainians who engaged in armed resis-

full-strength division. Order by Army Group Rear Area Center, September 2, 1942, *ibid.*, RII 22/233.

36. High Command of the Army/Org. II to all commands on the eastern front, August 1942, *ibid.*, RH 19 III/1942. The word "Turkic" in this designation was a greatly expanded version of the common linguistic term, in that several Caucasian nationalities, notably Georgians and Armenians, that are not Turkic were included.

37. Directive by Himmler, July 25, 1941, *ibid.*, RH 41/4.

38. See the Reich Security Main Office Operational Report No. 12, July 4, 1941, Nuremberg trials document NO-4529.

tance behind the German lines were also called "partisans." As a consequence, the word was banned from German official vocabulary. Soviet opponents in the German rear were henceforth "bands" (*Banden*).[39] Complicating things some more were non-Communist partisans who pursued independence from the Soviet Union and Germany alike. One ranking German Security Police officer called the Latvians in this category "chauvinists."[40]

In the concentration-camp world, a completely separate terminology was instituted for the many different kinds of prisoners. The term "concentration camp" (*Konzentrationslager,* abbreviated KL) was reserved for permanent installations under an inspectorate that was later incorporated into the SS Economic-Administrative Main Office. Most Jewish camp deaths occurred in Bełżec, Sobibór, Treblinka, and Kulmhof, which were rudimentary facilities under the control of regional Higher SS and Police Leaders, and which were not officially "concentration camps." The regular concentration-camp complex did include Auschwitz and Lublin (Maydanek in Polish), where Jews were killed, as well as several other camps that had Jewish inmates before the onset of full-scale

39. "Banden" are mentioned in an order of the 707th Division, December 22, 1941, National Archives, Record Group 242, T 315, Roll 2246. For "bandits," see Slovak Division/Ia, October 1 and 16, 1942, *ibid.,* T 315, Roll 2300. When SS and Police forces were sent out to areas that were "infested by bands" (*bandenverseucht*), Jews were killed automatically. By 1942 it became the fashion to list both Jewish dead and partisan dead in the reports under the rubric of "combatting bands" (*Bandenkampf*). A crass example is the report of the Higher SS and Police Leader of Ukraine (Hans-Adolf Prützmann) of December 26, 1942, whose numbers were an aggregate of 24,158 "bandits" and their helpers killed in action or "executed" after capture, and 363,211 "executed" Jews. National Archives, Record Group 242, T 175, Roll 124.

40. Commander (*Befehlshaber*) of Security Police in the Ostland (the Baltic area and western Byelorussia) to Reichskommissar of the Ostland, June 17, 1943, Lithuanian State Archives, Fond 1173, Opis 2, Folder 15.

gassing operations and again during the last year of the war. Three breakdowns were employed to sort prisoners in the concentration camps: one by nationality, another by the nature of the arrest (*Haftart*), and the third by the function or rank of the prisoner.

In a compilation of nationalities at the Dachau concentration camp in April 1945, which represents the fullest development of Nazi conceptualizations, the list of nationalities contained, among others, "Russians," "Lithuanians," "Serbs," "Slovaks," "Czechs," and even "Lorraines" (*Lothringer*). One small group was stateless. Jews and Gypsies were not nationalities at all but "Haftarten," i.e., causes of arrest.[41]

The principal arrest category was called "*Schutzhaft*" (Protective Custody). The beneficiary of the protection in this case was the state, not the prisoner. The arresting authority of protective custody prisoners (*Schutzhäftlinge*) was primarily the Secret State Police (*Geheime Staatspolizei*), known by its acronym as the Gestapo (Office IV of the Reich Security Main Office), but in mass roundups of Jews, particularly outside of Germany, the available personnel of various agencies were often pressed into service. The Schutzhäftlinge were divided into political prisoners (marked with a red triangle in the camps), homosexuals (pink), Jehovah's Witnesses (violet), and almost all Jews (yellow). A second arrest basis comprised the criminals (green) and "asocials" (black). Both were delivered to the camps by the Criminal Police (*Kriminalpolizei*, abbreviated Kripo). The greens were subdivided into habitual felons (*Berufsverbrecher*), whose camp incarceration was an addendum to a completed prison sentence, and so-called *Sicherungsverwahrte*, who were forced to serve their sentence in a camp rather than in prison. The "asocials" (*Asoziale*) were

---

41. Barbara Distel and Ruth Jakusch, eds., *Concentration Camp Dachau 1933–1945* (Brussels and Munich, 1978), p. 215.

a broad group, including those who repeatedly transgressed the law in minor ways, such as beggars, alcoholics, or itinerants, and those with or without a criminal record who were "work-shy" (*arbeitsscheu*). In a deviation from common practice, *Arbeitsscheue* were seized in 1938 in an action not by the Kripo but by the Gestapo. Also that year, Gypsies in the Sachsenhausen camp were a subcategory of Arbeitsscheue.[42]

For the stratification of inmates the SS employed an elaborate hierarchy of inmate overseers who wielded considerable power when camps became crowded, diseases rampant, and odors pungent. The highest positions in this auxiliary were filled with German prisoners, both red and green. There were two rank structures, one for territorial supervisors, the other for work parties. Inmates in charge of huts were called, from the top, *Lagerältester* (camp elder) for a section of a camp, *Blockältester* (block elder) for a barracks (known as "block" in camp language), and *Stubendienst* for a section of a barracks. Given the masses of inmates, a single barracks could hold five hundred inmates, often eight hundred or more. For work details, the ranks were *Oberkapo, Kapo,* and *Vorarbeiter* (foreman). The word "elder" did not mean a person of advanced age. Most of the elders were strong, young individuals. Kapos in most cases were not specialists or skilled but disciplinary au-

---

42. See the glossary and chronology in Martin Weinmann, ed., *Das nationalsozialistische Lagersystem* (Frankfurt am Main, 1990), pp. ix–lxxxiv. For color schemes, see Nationale Mahn- und Gedenkstätte Buchenwald, *Konzentrationslager Buchenwald* (East Berlin, 1990), p. 23. On "asocials" and criminals, see Wolfgang Ayass, "'Ein Gebot der nationalen Arbeitsdisziplin'—Die Aktion 'Arbeitsscheu Reich' 1938," and Patrick Wagner, "Das Gesetz über die Behandlung Gemeinschaftsfremder," in Ayass, *et al.*, *Feinderklärung und Prävention* (Berlin, 1988), pp. 43–100. On Gestapo action of 1938, see Döring, *Zigeuner,* pp. 56–58. A Sachsenhausen statistic of Gypsies is in Nationale Mahn- und Gedenkstätte Sachsenhausen Archives, R 021, Mappe 3, November 10, 1938.

thorities. Both elders and Kapos were free to beat prisoners, occasionally to death. Among inmates without ranks there was yet another advantaged population. These were the people with specified functions (*Funktionshäftlinge*), including the record keepers (*Schreiber*), physicians, and interpreters.[43]

For an emaciated inmate whose strength and will to live were nearing exhaustion, various camps had their own names. In Auschwitz it was a *Muselmann* (Moslem),[44] in the womens' camp Ravensbrück a *Muselweib* (deprecatory for Moslem woman), in Maydanek a *Gamel* (based on *Kamel*, or camel), in Buchenwald a *müder Scheich* (tired sheik), in Dachau a *Kretiner* (cretan), in Mauthausen a *Krüppel* (cripple), and in Neuengamme a *Schwimmer* (swimmer).[45]

Special words were adopted not only for the classification of persons. Sometimes they characterized actions. One example was the common word *Befreiung* (liberation) for the technical step of upgrading the status of Jew to a Mischling, or more often of a Mischling to German. A Befreiung was "genuine" (*echt*) if it was based on the "merit" of the recipient, and not genuine (*unecht*) if it was merely the correction of a factual error pertaining to the person's descent.[46]

Another illustration is the word "Aryanization" (*Arisierung*) to describe the transfer of a Jewish firm into "Aryan" hands. As in the case of the words "Jews" and "Aryans," the "Aryan" firm was the one that was not Jewish; it

---

43. See Wolfgang Sofsky, *Die Ordnung des Terrors: Das Konzentrationslager* (Frankfurt am Main, 1993), pp. 152–168. In camps with sections for women, female inmates occupied such positions.

44. Obersturmführer (SS 1st Lieutenant) Heinrich Schwarz to SS Economic-Administrative Main Office/DII, on transfer of inmates from Dachau to Auschwitz, October 30, 1942, facsimile in Distel and Jakusch, *Dachau*, p. 132. Schwarz was in charge of labor allocation in Auschwitz.

45. Sofsky, *Ordnung des Terrors*, pp. 152–168, and p. 363 n. 5.

46. See Stuckart and Schiedermair, *Rasse- und Erbpflege*, pp. 18–19.

was the "Jewish" firm that had to be defined.[47] In Romania an office of "Romanianization," the *Centrul Naţional de Romanizare*, concerned itself with the replacement of Jewish laborers by Romanians.[48]

A third special term was the word *Einzelaktionen*, which was officially defined as "all measures" that did not "rest on explicit directives of the Reich Government or [Central] Reich directives of the National Socialist German Workers Party."[49] The concept was formulated because the business sector, and particularly Reichsbank President Hjalmar Schacht, complained about street violence and molestations of German shoppers in Jewish stores.[50] This behavior was henceforth prohibited. Even though a large-scale action of smashing the windows of Jewish shops and burning the synagogues erupted during the night of November 9–10, 1938, after veiled oral orders had been sent out by Propaganda Minister Goebbels,[51] the "Crystal Night," as it became known, was the last occurrence of this nature on German soil. Thereafter the emphasis on orderly process, which had been stressed by Hitler himself as early as 1919,[52] prevailed as a fundamental principle of anti-Jewish action until the end of the war.

Some words, found in everyday language, had not been assigned a specific meaning for an operational purpose, but in

47. Decree of June 14, 1938, RGBl I, 627.

48. For the text of the law in German and Romanian, an organization chart, and leading personnel, see National Archives, Record Group 242, T 175, Roll 659.

49. Compilation of letters by the Economy Ministry, October 10, 1935; Interior Ministry, October 25, 1935; and the Deputy of the Führer (Rudolf Hess), October 31, 1935, to Reich Industry Association, T 71, Roll 127.

50. See summary of Schacht conference, August 22, 1935, Nuremberg trials document NG-4067.

51. Walter Buch (chief of Nazi party court) to Hermann Göring, February 13, 1939, Nuremberg trials document PS-3063.

52. Letter of Hitler, September 16, 1919, in Ernst Deuerlein, ed., *Der Aufstieg der NSDAP in Augenzeugenberichten* (Munich, 1974), pp. 91–94.

certain contexts they were virtually indispensable to convey a particular policy, attitude, or assessment. An example is the commonplace adjective *selbstverständlich*, meaning self-evident, a matter of course, obvious, to be taken for granted, requiring no stated reason. For a ranking official of the Education Ministry, it was "selbstverständlich" that a German, and especially a Nazi party member, was not supposed to buy anything from a Jew.[53] Similarly, for a German intelligence officer it was "selbstverständlich" that German soldiers maintain an attitude of ruthlessness and distance vis-à-vis Jewish forced laborers.[54] Equally "selbstverständlich" was the norm that there could be no communal relationship between Germans and Poles.[55] When Reinhard Heydrich, Chief of the Reich Security Main Office, was asked by one of his officers just before the onslaught on the USSR whether the Jews should be killed, Heydrich is reported to have replied "selbstverständlich."[56] Again, in two directives written after this meeting, Heydrich used the word four times in connection with the identification of two groups in the newly conquered territory, one which might be useful, the other to be shot.[57] "Selbstverständlich"

53. Summary of letter by Staatssekretär Zschintzsch to Chief of the Reich Chancellery Hans Lammers, December 24, 1937, in official diary of Justice Minister Gürtner, January 3, 1939, National Archives, Record Group 238, M 978, Roll 3.

54. Report by Oberleutnant Werner Scheibe, 493rd Security Division, Ia, for July 1941, *ibid.*, Record Group 242, T 315, Roll 2206.

55. Information sheet of the Gauleitung press office in the Wartheland, March 16, 1942, facsimile in Diemut Majer, *"Fremdvölkische" im Dritten Reich* (Boppard am Rhein, 1981), following p. 128.

56. Summary of interrogation of Karl Jäger, June 15, 1959, in Landeskriminalamt Baden-Württemberg, Sonderkommission/Zentrale Stelle, I/3-2/59. Jäger, commander of Einsatzkommando 3 in 1941, had been returned from Soviet captivity.

57. Heydrich to commanders of Einsatzgruppen, July 1 and 2, 1941, German Federal Archives, R 70 SU/32. In each directive the word was used twice.

appears in German correspondence over and over, and in virtually every case it was a signal that explicit reasons were unnecessary.

Also valued was the word *radikal,* which in German parlance of the time had the meaning that surgeons assign to "radical" procedures in the operating room. In January 1940, Dr. Leonardo Conti, the Staatssekretär in the Interior Ministry responsible for health, advocated as a *Radikallösung* (radical solution) the sterilization of Gypsies and Gypsy Mischlinge rather than their deportation to Poland, from where they might one day return to Germany.[58] In August 1941 an army officer in Byelorussia considered it advisable that his regiment proceed in a "more radical" (*radikaler*) manner against the rural Jews in his area,[59] and in May 1942 a general in Paris said that he always adopted a "radical point of view" (*radikalen Standpunkt*) in Jewish matters.[60]

Smooth operations, without unexpected incidents or obstacles, were often styled *reibungslos* (literally, without friction). A police lieutenant in the field used the word in recounting two of his shooting expeditions in western sections of Byelorussia.[61] Eichmann used it for deportations from France.[62] In diplomatic correspondence the deportations from

58. Conti's memorandum is cited by Zimmermann, *Rassenutopie,* p. 171.

59. Generalmajor Hellmuth Koch, commander of 350th Infantry Regiment, to 221st Security Division, National Archives, Record Group 242, T 315, Roll 1672. Koch endorsed the recommendation of an unnamed officer.

60. The general was Otto Kohl. Hauptsturmführer (SS Captain) Theodor Dannecker to Standartenführer (SS Colonel) Helmut Knochen in Paris, May 13, 1942, in Serge Klarsfeld, ed., *Die Endlösung der Judenfrage in Frankreich* (Paris, 1977), p. 56.

61. Bezirksleutnant der Gendarmerie Max Eibner via Gendarmerie-Hauptmannschaft to Kommandeur der Gendarmerie in Byelorussia, August 26, 1942, Zentrale Stelle der Landesjustizverwaltungen in Ludwigsburg, UdSSR 245c.

62. Memorandum signed by Eichmann and Dannecker, August 1, 1942, in Klarsfeld, *Endlösung in Frankreich,* pp. 71–72.

Hungary were also "reibungslos,"[63] and the railroads closed the Treblinka station to regular passenger traffic in order to assure the "reibungslose" processing of four Jewish transports to the camp.[64]

In communicating with a conquered population, German rulers frequently used vocabulary with which they could stress their power and the corresponding powerlessness of the inhabitants. Authority and its capabilities called for the use of *Verwaltung* (administration), *Behörde* (an administrative body dealing with the public), *Genehmigung* (official permission), *beglaubigen* (certify), *Befehl* (order), *Wehrmachtsangehörige* (members of the armed forces), *Stützpunkt* (military base), *Sicherheit* (security), and *rücksichtslos* (without consideration, ruthless). The weakness of the civilian population was emphasized in the words *verhaften* (arrest), *ausfragen* (interrogate), *schuldig* (guilty), and *zwecklos* (useless, as in useless petitions and useless resistance). Disapproval was expressed in *Bande* (referring to partisans), *Aufwiegler* (rabble-rouser), *Aufruhr* (disorder), *Frechheit* (impudence), and *Schwätzer* (babbler, especially rumormonger). All these words, and more, were included in lists of a basic German vocabulary published in a Ukrainian-language newspaper of the occupied city of Kamenets Podolsky.[65]

Some expressions were shared by perpetrators and victims.

63. The German minister in Hungary, reporting a conversation with Hungarian Interior Minister Andor Jaross, to Foreign Office, July 9, 1944, Nuremberg trials document NG-5532.

64. Generaldirektor der Ostbahn/33 (special trains division) to stations en route from Siedlce to Ostrołęka, Zentrale Stelle Ludwigsburg, Collection Polen, Film 6.

65. United States Holocaust Memorial Museum Archives, Accession No. 1996 A 0150 (Khmelnitsky Oblast Archives), Roll 6. The newspaper, known as *Der Podolier* in German, carried the lists of approximately twenty-five to twenty-seven words daily for a few months, starting in February 1942.

An example is *Protektion,* which in the Netherlands, as in *Protektionsjuden,* referred to Jews spared from deportation to a death camp because of a recognized status,[66] and which in the Slavic-Yiddish version *protektsia,* current in eastern Europe, had a wider connotation of an advantage held by those Jews who could rely on a connection with influential Jewish functionaries or potentates. The term "organize" was used by inmates of Auschwitz with reference to stealing something in a depot or kitchen.[67] The same word was used by the SS and Police Leader of Galicia to describe the work of Jews who were knowledgeable enough in the ways of the black market to find scarce materials for German needs in the underground economy.[68] In Ukraine, however, where German soldiers regularly resorted to *organisieren* whenever they helped themselves to something, the military commander forbade the word, since it was only a "cover to beautify punishable acts."[69]

BLUNT AND BLUNTED LANGUAGE

The hallmark of a bureaucracy is functionalism and professionalism; its typical attitude is that of detachment; and the manner of its language, reinforced with special and specialized

66. Gertrud Slottke (Gestapo) to Sturmbannführer (SS Major) Wilhelm Zoepf, November 3, 1942, National Archives, Record Group 242, T 175, Roll 671. See also *Prominente* in Theresienstadt, in H. G. Adler, *Theresienstadt* (Tübingen, 1960), pp. 310–312.

67. For example, Gisella Perl, *I Was a Doctor in Auschwitz* (New York, 1948), p. 76.

68. Report by SS and Police Leader Fritz Katzmann in Galicia, Nuremberg trials document L-18.

69. Order by Wehrmachtbefehlshaber Ukraine, January 6, 1942, United States Holocaust Memorial Archives, Accession No. 1996 A 269 (Zhitomir Oblast Archives), Roll 2, Fond 1151, Opis 1, Folder 21.

words, allows discussion of all sorts of matters in the same un-
feeling tone. That course, however, was not followed in every
situation. At one time or another the style of some utterances
became markedly graphic and outspoken, and in others it was
roundabout. Writers usually had a special reason when they
referred to a concrete subject in either of these modes.

Bluntness is accentuated articulation. Not merely clear and
succinct, it is immediately recognizable, whether in a sentence
or on a crowded page in a voluminous exchange of messages.
Occasions for the use of such prose arose when its author
wanted to underscore a point, as in a suggestion, or when
someone in authority demanded unprecedented action at a
particular juncture, or when a witness became critical or the
writer of a report self-congratulatory, or when someone cast
an encompassing backward glance at all that had happened.

At an early stage of the Nazi regime, in 1934, a subordinate of Security Service Chief Heydrich introduced a set of
detailed proposals in the following manner:

> Jews must be deprived of their potential for a life—not
> only in the economic sphere. Germany must be a land
> without a future for them. Only the old generation should
> be allowed to die here in peace, but not the young, so that
> the incentive to emigrate remains. As a means, rowdy anti-
> Semitism is to be rejected. One does not combat rats with
> the revolver, but with poison and gas. The foreign reper-
> cussions of street methods far outweigh any local success.[70]

---

70. Security Service IV/2 to Heydrich, May 24, 1934, printed in
Michael Wildt, ed., *Die Judenpolitik des SD 1935 bis 1938* (Munich, 1995),
pp. 66–69. Wildt, citing the Center for the Preservation of Historical Documentary Collections, Moscow, Fond 501, Opis 1, Folder 18, identifies the
chief of IV/2 and probable author of the memorandum as retired army
major Walter Ilges.

In January 1938 a ranking corporate officer of the Friedrich Flick concern, Otto Steinbrinck, writing about the difficulties involved in a hostile takeover of the large Jewish-owned Ignatz Petschek coal enterprise, considered the possible necessity of resorting to "measures of force or interventions of the state" (*Gewaltmassnahmen oder staatliche Eingriffe*).[71]

By 1943 a German official in the central Polish region comprising the Generalgouvernement weighed a long-range course of action vis-à-visa the fifteen million Poles in his area. Rejecting plenary solutions, such as the Germanization of this Polish population, or its total expulsion, or the "radical cure" of "elimination" (an option he regarded as "unworthy" of a civilized nation), he proposed in "magnanimous" fashion the Germanization of seven or eight million, the employment in manual labor of several million more, and the "unavoidable" application of "radical means" to two or three million Polish "fanatics," "asocials," and ailing or worthless people.[72]

Quite different from the advisory role of these men, who expressed their thoughts with deliberation, was the position of the Romanian dictator Marshal Ion Antonescu, at the close of 1941. The Romanians had joined Germany in the invasion of the Soviet Union, sustaining heavy casualties. They had then expelled Jews from newly conquered regions, causing massive Jewish losses, and when the Romanian military headquarters was blown up in captured Odessa, Antonescu gave orders to kill Jews in the tens of thousands. Finally, on De-

71. Memorandum by Steinbrinck, January 10, 1938, Nuremberg trials document NI-3254.

72. Text of the document, authored by Friedrich Gollert, March 29, 1943, in Susanne Heim and Götz Aly, eds., *Bevölkerungsstruktur und Massenmord* (Berlin, 1991), pp. 145–151. The original is in the YIVO Institute (New York), document Occ E 2–74.

cember 16, 1941, Antonescu spoke about the Jewish inhabitants who were still alive in that city:

> Are we waiting for something to be decided in Berlin? Are we waiting for a decision that concerns us? We have to put them in a secure place. Stick them in catacombs, stick them in the Black Sea, but remove them from Odessa. I do not want to know anything. A hundred can die, a thousand can die, all can die . . .[73]

Antonescu's outburst, in the course of a meeting, was impulsive. That was not the situation when Sturmbannführer (SS-Major) Gustav Lombard, who commanded the 1st SS Cavalry Regiment, in the Pripet Marshes, was confronted with Himmler's order of August 1, 1941, to shoot Jewish men and to drive Jewish women into the swamps. Lombard, who had to pass these instructions to his men that day, noted that Himmler's admonition was not a criticism of the unit, because there happened to have been no Jews in its sector, except for two villages where they were urgently needed as workers. "Nevertheless," Lombard added, "leaders of reconnaissance squads especially are to be sharply reminded again. No Jew remains alive, no remnant families in the towns."[74]

73. See Radu Ioanid, "When Mass Murderers Become Good Men," *Journal of Holocaust Education*, vol. 4 (1995), pp. 22–104, on p. 101. The full Romanian text is in United States Holocaust Memorial Museum Archives, Record Group 25.004 (Serviciul Roman de Informaţii), Roll 34, Fond 40010, vol. 1.

74. Order by Lombard, August 1, 1941, German Federal Archives, RS 4/441. No less outspoken was an order prohibiting the rash shooting of laborers who had no connections to partisans. "The general has ordered that in principle no work forces are to be shot" (*Herr General befiehlt dass grundsätzlich keine Arbeitskräfte zu erschiessen sind*). Kommandantur in Smolensk/Ia to Gruppenkommando in Tishino, February 25, 1942, United States Holocaust Memorial Museum Archives, Record Group 48.004 (Military Historical Archives, Prague), Roll 2, Collection Polizei Regiment Mitte, K 8-11.

Most Jews of Vilnius were shot in the summer and fall of 1941, mainly in the Ponary Forest south of the city. On January 1, 1942, the following manifesto written by a twenty-two-year-old organizer in a resistance group, Abba Kovner, was proclaimed:

> Ponar means death. Those who waver, put aside all illusions. Your children, your wives, and husbands are no more. Ponar is no concentration camp. All were shot dead there. Hitler conspires to kill all the Jews of Europe, and the Jews of Lithuania have been picked as the first in line. Let us not be led like sheep to the slaughter![75]

The last phrase, which was used on following occasions in Warsaw and Bialystok,[76] actually inverts the meaning of Psalm 44, in which Jews are told not to rely on bow and sword. They are delivered like sheep to the slaughter by the Lord, and to the Lord they are to call out for deliverance.

The violent Antonescu, the emphatic Lombard, and the fiery Kovner were men of will whose words broke the mold. Their utterances were not idle. Antonescu brought about the subsequent deaths of tens of thousands, Lombard's regiment went on to shoot many thousands, and Kovner became an armed partisan who commanded a group of escaping Jews.

Bystanders at a scene sometimes adopted an openly critical tone. A professional Jewish writer in the Warsaw ghetto, Jehuszua Perle, who made a statement for the Jewish underground archives, had difficulty saying what he had just

75. See text in Yizhak Arad, *Ghetto in Flames* (New York, 1982), pp. 231–232. There is also a longer version.

76. See the proclamations issued by the left-of-center Jewish underground organization and that of its right-wing counterpart, both in Warsaw, in Yitzhak Arad, Yisrael Gutman, and Abraham Margaliot, eds., *Documents on the Holocaust* (Jerusalem, 1981), pp. 301–303. The phrase appeared again in a proclamation in the Bialystok ghetto. Text in Jüdisches Historisches Institut Warschau, *Faschismus-Getto-Massenmord*, pp. 558–559.

observed. He noted the march of two hundred silent Jewish children from their orphanage and added: "Here I must repeat the banal words that there is no pen with which to describe this horrible picture."[77] A Polish policeman did not wrestle for words. Talking to an ethnic German woman about Jewish children whose heads had been trampled, he asked her whether she was not ashamed. The woman, disturbed by what she had heard, recapitulated this conversation in an anonymous letter that reached the Reich Chancellery in Berlin.[78] An operations officer of the 403rd Security Division wrote on July 16, 1941, about men who acted with "brutal ruthlessness" (*mit brutaler Rücksichtslosigkeit*), adding that "their hatred of Poles and Jews requires supervision." He was referring to Lithuanians.[79]

A German police sergeant in charge of a guard detachment accompanying a mammoth transport of some 8,000 Jews from Kolomea to the death camp of Bełżec concluded his description of incident after incident with the following evaluation: "The ever increasing panic among the Jews brought about by intense heat, overcrowding of up to 220 Jews in cars, the stench of corpses—there were about 2,000 dead inside the wagons—made the transport an almost impossible task."[80] In this kind of "what it was like" account there is a double-edged meaning: the Jews were desperate, but he too had reached a

77. Text in *Faschismus-Getto-Massenmord, ibid.*, pp. 313–314.

78. Anonymous letter sent via Generalgouverneur Frank to Hitler and received in the Reich Chancellery on March 25, 1943, Nuremberg trials document NG-1903.

79. War Diary of 403rd Security Division/Ia, July 16, 1941, National Archives, Record Group 242, T 315, Roll 2206.

80. Report by Zugwachtmeister Jäcklein (7th Company, 24th Police Regiment), who commanded the transport detachment, September 14, 1942, United States Holocaust Memorial Museum Archives, Record Group 11.001 (Center for Historical Documentary Collections, Moscow), Roll 82, Fond 1323, Opis 2, Folder 2926.

limit, so let no one think this was an excursion. An SS Standartenführer (colonel) farther north, who sent a tabulation of 133,346 dead for which he took credit, added an explanation of his difficulties in a spirit of accomplishment. The Jews had to be marched, on average, about three miles from collecting points to the ditches. It was nerve-racking work. Vehicles were seldom available, and escapes were frustrated by his men at the risk of their lives, and so forth.[81]

Unvarnished language was used not only by initiators of action, or by those who witnessed or passed on reports of specific events that surpassed normal experience. It was also employed at moments of reflection on the sweep of events. In October 1943, when Himmler noticed that a door was open at a gathering of his ranking subordinates, he instructed a guard to close it, for what he was about to say was not intended for unauthorized ears. Then, in the middle of his long talk about a wide range of subjects, he mentioned a hundred bodies lying there or five hundred there, or a thousand, and what it meant to have "gone through this."[82] In such inner circles, reflection would sometimes be expressed in a tone of finality. "One must not have mercy with people who are determined by fate to perish," said Hitler at the dinner table on April 2, 1942.[83] "The Jews are doomed whether we do or we don't," wrote Morris Waldman, an official of the American Jewish Committee, on May 19, 1943.[84]

81. Report by Standartenführer Karl Jäger, December 1, 1941, Center for the Preservation of Historical Documentary Collections, Moscow, Fond 500, Opis 1, Folder 25.

82. Speech by Himmler, October 4, 1943, Nuremberg trials document PS-1919. The entire speech is on audiotape in the National Archives, Record Group 242.

83. Henry Picker, ed., *Hitlers Tischgespräche im Führerhauptquartier 1941–1942* (Bonn, 1951), p. 277. The entries are summaries by Picker.

84. Waldman to Josef Proskauer of the Committee, May 19, 1943, Archives of the American Jewish Committee, EXO-29, Waldman files.

Next to direct approach that could not fail to elicit immediate attention, one may also find its opposite: veiled language. The dimming of a disclosure was not meant to produce
an opaque or ambiguous message, because the intended recipient had to understand what was said. Rather, it was a carefully
chosen formulation that would be transparent enough to the
initiated reader. The practice, which at times was prompted
less by a need to preserve secrets from outsiders than a desire
to guard one's own conscience, may be divided into three variants. The first was the varnish of legitimization. The second
was a primitive code. The third consisted of more elaborate,
circuitous phraseology.

A simple way of covering an act with the gloss of the law
was a formula used by the 1st SS Brigade for the mass shooting of Jews: "Actions according to the customs of war" (*Aktio-
nen nach Kriegsbrauch*).[85] Another example is a proclamation
issued by the commander of the Eleventh Army, Walter von
Reichenau, to his troops: "Therefore, the soldiers must have
full understanding for the hard but just retribution visited on
Jewish subhumanity."[86] Almost without thinking, a defendant
before a German court as late as 1966 described shootings in
Ljepaja, Latvia, as follows: "Most of the delinquents wore a
yellow Jewish star on their clothes. . . . Among the delinquents
were men, women, and children."[87]

As for code words, there was an array of euphemisms,

85. See reports of the brigade to the Command Staff (Kommandostab)
of the SS in United States Holocaust Memorial Museum Archives, Record
Group 48.004 (Military Historical Archives, Prague), Roll 1. In the report
of November 28, 1941, the phrase was actually set off in quotes. I am grateful to Robert Kunath for calling this oddity to my attention.

86. Order by Reichenau, October 10, 1941, National Archives, Record
Group 242, T 315, Roll 984.

87. Statement by Carl Emil Strott before Landgericht Hannover in the
case against Georg Rosenstock, March 4, 1966, UR 6/64, xi, 1380, renum-
bered 2442.

some of which suggested the removal of harmful Jewish parasites or vermin, like "cleansing" (*Säuberung*),[88] "Dejewification measures" (*Entjudungsmassnahmen*),[89] and "made free of Jews" (*judenfrei gemacht*).[90] A much-used prefix was *Sonder-* (special). In Auschwitz, where killing could hardly be hidden from anyone for an extended period, an architect of the SS Central Construction Staff called three projected barracks that were to hold the personal belongings of gassed Jews "effects barracks for special treatment" (*Effektenbaracke für Sonderbehandlung 3 Stück*).[91] The underground gas chambers were styled "special cellars" (*Sonderkeller*), and surface chambers were called "bath houses for special actions" (*Badeanstalten für Sonderaktionen*).[92] For Himmler the word "Sonderbehandlung" was overused by 1943. Dictating a change in a draft report by the SS statistician Richard Korherr, he ordered the substitution "sluiced through" (*durchgeschleust*) the death camps of the Generalgouvernement.[93]

The discussion of sensitive matters could require more than camouflaging words. Whole passages or even entire mes-

88. See report by Orskommandantur Kakhovka, October 20, 1941, National Archives, Record Group 242, T 501, Roll 56. The report is about a killing.

89. See Report No. 93 of the Commander (Befehlshaber) of Security Police in the Netherlands, May 12, 1942, *ibid.*, T 175, Roll 670. The report is about deportations.

90. Report by Commander (Kommandeur) of Security Police in Lithuania, Standartenführer (SS Colonel) Wilhelm Fuchs, April 30, 1943, Central State Archives of Lithuania, Fond 1399, Opis 1, Folder 26.

91. Memorandum by Untersturmführer (SS 2nd Lieutenant) Fritz Ertl, June 3, 1942, United States Holocaust Memorial Museum Archives, Record Group 11.001 (Center for the Preservation of Historical Documentary Collections, Moscow), Roll 35, Fond 501, Opis 1, Folder 2236.

92. Memoranda by Ertl, November 27 and August 21, 1942, *ibid.*, Roll 41, Fond 502, Opis 1, Folder 313.

93. Himmler's adjutant Rudolf Brandt to Korherr, April 10, 1943, Nuremberg trials document NO-5195.

sages were drafted to transmit information in a verbal dis-
guise. Himmler was a master of such communications. The
following two orders, which he issued, were about one year
apart, but they were in close proximity to his concerns. The
first, dated December 12, 1941, is less shaded than the second.
It was sent to his Higher SS and Police Leaders in the occupied USSR and distributed to lower echelons. There the SS
and Police had already shot approximately a half-million people.

The task assigned to us, to guarantee security, tranquility,
and order in the territories entrusted to us, particularly in
the rear of the German frontline, demands that we remove
every locus of rebellion and convey every enemy of the
German people to a just punishment of death.

A holy duty of highly placed leaders and commanders it
is to ensure personally that none of our men who have to
fulfill this heavy duty, succumb or suffer damage to their
spirit and character. This task is fulfilled with the sharpest
discipline enforced by those encumbered with the responsibility, and through comradely togetherness during the
evening of a day that brought with it such a difficult task.
The comradely togetherness, however, must never end
with misuse of alcohol. It should be an evening that—possibilities permitting—is filled, while sitting and eating at a
table, with music, lectures, and the transport of our men to
the finer areas of German intellectual and spiritual life.

I consider timely replacement of burdened Kommandos, and timely furloughs as well as transfers to other
tasks—possibly to another region—that will fulfill a man
fully and completely, as important and urgent.

Equally, however, I wish that in essence it be deemed
impossible and improper to discuss or converse about facts

and related numbers. Orders and duties must be carried out that are necessary for the life of a people. Afterward, they are not, however, the stuff of talk and conversation.[94]

Himmler addressed himself to the subject of killing operations again in November 1942, after he had become aware of rumors in the United States about the processing of bodies into soap. Reports to this effect had been sent out from Europe during the summer, and they reached the president of the World Jewish Congress, Rabbi Stephen Wise.[95] Himmler in turn had been alerted to a memorandum by Wise. Although the rumors were false, Himmler was not totally confident that he could dismiss the matter altogether. He therefore wrote the following instructions to his Gestapo chief, Heinrich Müller:

> In the enclosure, I am sending you a very interesting report about a memorandum by Dr. Stephen Wise of September 1942.
>
> That rumors of this kind are circulating worldwide does not surprise me, considering the large emigration movement of the Jews. We both know that among the Jews employed in labor there is a heightened mortality rate.
>
> You have to guarantee that in every place the bodies of Jews who died are either burned or buried, and that in no place anything else could happen with the bodies.

94. Himmler to Higher SS and Police Leaders, with downward distribution in the East, December 12, 1941, Latvian State Archives, Fond 83, Opis 1, Folder 80.

95. Gerhart Riegner (World Jewish Congress representative in Geneva) to Rabbi Irving Miller (secretary-general of the World Jewish Congress), August 28, 1942, citing a report of an unnamed non-Jewish Pole in Switzerland of August 13, American Jewish Archives, World Jewish Congress Collection, Alphabetical Files Switzerland 184-A, #1, Warnings 1942-43, I-k. See also Monty Noam Penkower, *The Jews Were Expendable* (Urbana, Ill., 1983), pp. 67–81.

Find out at once whether there was anywhere any misuse such as the one in Point 1, undoubtedly disseminated to the world as a lie. Every misuse of that kind is to be reported to me on SS-oath.[96]

Auschwitz was a camp with multiple functions. One was industrial production, for which inmate labor was used extensively; but Jews, who constituted the large majority of all the incoming prisoners, were subject to gassing, either immediately upon arrival or periodically after selection from the inmate population. As of August 1943, the four newly built gas chamber–crematorium units were in operation, and the cumulative total of Jewish dead had already reached several hundred thousand. The industrialists in Auschwitz were concerned about the conservation of their Jewish labor, and the following excerpt from a memorandum by an SS officer summarizes an Auschwitz meeting about this matter:

> A special apprehension was voiced by Director Wielan: one might have to assume that owing to possible necessities of a political or police nature, trained inmate personnel, or inmate laborers altogether, could be withdrawn, and that thereby the continuity of production could be disturbed by delay.
>
> SS-Hauptsturmführer [Captain] Schwarz expressed assurance of special priority in the allocation of inmate skilled labor and described the aforesaid changes as unlikely.[97]

96. Himmler to Müller, November 10, 1942, National Archives, Record Group 242, T 175, Roll 18.

97. Memorandum by Untersturmführer Hans Kirschneck, August 23, 1943, United States Holocaust Memorial Museum Archives, Record Group 11.001 (Center for the Preservation of Historical Documentary Collections, Moscow), Roll 20, Fond 502, Opis 1, Folder 26. Wielan, an industrialist, represented Special Committee Munitions III of the Armaments Ministry.

The technique of avoiding outspoken language was practiced also by Jews. The protocol of a Jewish community meeting in Berlin, dated September 28, 1942, refers to 1,058 deportees on a transport that left two days earlier as "participants" (*Teilnehmer*).[98] In the Łódź ghetto, which was the second largest in Poland, the Jewish "Elder," Chaim Rumkowski, employed several writers to keep a daily chronicle of events. The ghetto, formed in 1940, had lost a substantial part of its population in two waves of deportations in 1942. By the beginning of 1944 its 80,000 remaining inhabitants worked in shifts day and night. From time to time official German visitors, including auditors, would appear in the Jewish Council offices at the Baluty Circle. On January 16, 1944, one of the chroniclers, Oskar Rosenfeld, entered the following paragraph under the heading of "Daily Reports" in the log:

> The Commission is still in the ghetto. The tension at the Baluty Ring continues and unrest spreads to the population. To all appearances, important decisions are being made. The population, however, is reduced to racking its brains about all the audits and statistical accounting.[99]

Rosenfeld also kept a personal diary, and this is his private notation on the same day about the same occurrence:

> January 16. Anxiety—Resettlement. Commission in ghetto. Demands statistical records of production in specific enterprises: hours, workers, maximum productivity, etc. At the same time, listing of all the machines in the

98. Protocol No. 19 of the meeting of the directorate of the Reichsvereinigung, Rabbi Leo Baeck presiding, September 28, 1942. Zentralarchiv (Central Archives of the German Democratic Republic), Potsdam, 75 c Re 1, Laufende Nummer 2. The report about the transport was presented by Philipp Kozower.

99. Excerpt from the daily chronicle in typescript, through the courtesy of Lucjan Dobroszycki.

ghetto. Possible evacuation of the ghetto in Sustne and also area all around because of developments at the front? No one knows anything definite, only this: Once again we face acute danger.[100]

In the United States, Adolph Held, president of the Jewish Labor Committee, wrote a memorandum about a meeting held on December 8, 1942, between five American Jewish leaders and President Roosevelt. The Jewish delegation had petitioned the president to make a public statement and gather more information about the fate of European Jewry. Millions of Jews were already dead, and even though the Jewish organizations had underestimated the number, they were conscious of the extreme peril confronting those who were still alive. Until that day these leaders had not met with the president face to face. Held described what happened in that half-hour by filling his summary with a great deal of minute, seemingly irrelevant detail.

The meeting began exactly at noon. The president was seated, smoking a cigarette, behind a desk "full of all sorts of trinkets, brass and porcelain figures, etc. There was not an empty spot on the desk." In the next paragraph he described the president's greeting of the delegation leader, Rabbi Wise. "How have you been, Stephen? You are looking well. Glad to see you looking well." When the delegates were seated, Roosevelt talked about his intention of appointing Governor Herbert Lehman of New York, who was Jewish, to become the head of a new Office of Relief and Rehabilitation, which would hand out bread to the Germans after the war. Roosevelt would want to watch that scene behind a curtain "with sadistic satisfaction." In the following paragraph, Held recounted a re-

100. Oskar Rosenfeld, *Wozu noch Welt* (Frankfurt am Main, 1994), p. 262. The ghetto was emptied out seven months later and Rosenfeld died in Auschwitz.

quest by Wise to permit the Orthodox rabbi in the delegation to offer a prayer. Wise then referred to a declaration by the committee, and Roosevelt pointed out that the government was already acquainted with the facts. The president, characterizing Hitler as insane, went on to say that it was too early "to make pronouncements such as President Wilson made," but that he would be glad to issue another statement.

The president then asked the delegation whether it had any suggestions. There were just a few. Held himself brought up the possibility of "getting some of the neutral representatives in Germany to intercede in behalf of the Jews." Roosevelt made no direct reply. The suggestions had taken up only a minute or two. "As a matter of fact," Held notes, "of the 29 minutes spent with the president, he addressed the delegation for 23 minutes."

Yet another paragraph was devoted to the president's additional remarks, which were about French North Africa. Roosevelt laid out American policy with respect to this area, most of which had been occupied by American troops during the previous month. Jews and Frenchmen, said Roosevelt, had possessed greater rights in parts of that region than Moslems, and Americans did not fight for inequality. Americans championed equal rights for all. The attack on Jews in Europe was an attack on American ideas of freedom and justice, "and that is why we oppose it so vehemently." After quoting a proverb he had heard from a Yugoslav priest about crossing one's bridge before quarreling with the devil, Roosevelt "must have pushed some secret button," and his adjutant appeared in the room. The president shook hands with his visitors and they were ushered out.[101]

Held's account was an office memorandum written in Yid-

---

101. Facsimile of the memorandum as translated from the Yiddish, in David Wyman, ed., *America and the Holocaust* (New York, 1990), I, 72–74.

dish, but no sentence in these fifteen hundred words was evaluative. The impact of Roosevelt's reactions is manifest solely in the portrayal of the small details. Overlooking nothing in the room, and timing every utterance in stopwatch fashion, Held leaves no doubt about the momentousness of the half-hour. The bric-a-brac on the desk had precluded at the outset that anything the delegates might say would be noted by the president on some pad of paper. The opening remark about Governor Lehman's postwar role was a shift of focus. The six minutes used by the delegation included a prayer, and the substantive conversation took a minute or two. Toward the end, Roosevelt coupled the situation of the Moslems in North Africa with that of the Jews in Europe. Finally, the imagined button symbolizes the end of the patently futile Jewish effort.

FLOURISHES

In an elaborate report prepared in the Jewish Council of Częstochowa for 1941, a designer drew figures of men and women in a demographic pyramid.[102] Farther to the north, in Riga, a German illustrator drew caskets on an outline map showing the record of killing by Einsatzgruppe A.[103] Decorations like these are relatively rare. More often a verbal adornment was offered, particularly for expressing a negative sentiment. In the main, four tools were used for this purpose: deliberate crudity, unexpected conjunctions, wordplay, and irony.

Documents contain no lack of raw words or phrases. They could be taken from propaganda slogans or from the spoken

---

102. United States Holocaust Memorial Museum Archives, Record Group 15.061 (Żydowski Instytut Historyczny), Roll 1, Records of the Jewish Council in Częstochowa.

103. Draft report of Einsatzgruppe A (end of January 1942), Nuremberg trials document PS-2273.

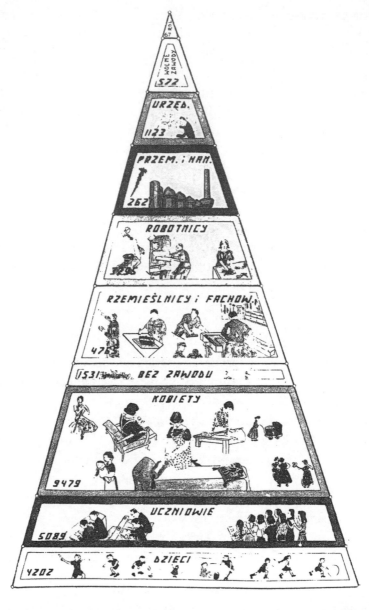

A demographic pyramid, prepared for the elaborate report of the
Jewish Council of Częstochowa for 1941.

Caskets on an outline map showing the record of killing by
Einsatzgruppe A, January 1942.

idiom of home, street, or gutter. Sometimes they were used by high-ranking officials in a jocular mood,[104] or, more seldom, in official correspondence. The chief of Himmler's Personal Staff, Karl Wolff, once thanked the Staatssekretär of the railroads, Albert Ganzenmüller, for expediting the transport of "the chosen people" to Treblinka,[105] and a noncommissioned officer of the army's Secret Field Police in charge of a detachment rounding up Jews in the Greek city of Ioánnina referred to the victims as "Hebrews" (*Hebräer*).[106] Some soldiers writing letters to wives and parents would cite the language of the virulent Nazi party newspaper *Der Stürmer*. Others, who did not know one another, used identical wording to say how Jews had affected their senses. The Jews stank or smelled of garlic. They were living in filth (*Dreck*) or were filthy (*dreckig*). The "Jew faces" were grotesque (*Fratzen*). It swarmed (*wimmelte*) of Jews. They were riffraff shunning light (*lichtscheues Gesindel*). They were or looked impudent (*frech*).[107]

104. For example, Hermann Göring in a conference under his chairmanship of November 12, 1938, *ibid.*, PS-1816. The record of the conference is verbatim. When conference summaries were prepared, such free expressions were omitted. See the testimony of Adolf Eichmann, who kept the minutes of the Final Solution conference of January 20, 1942, and who drafted the minutes, which were proofread by Reinhardt Heydrich. Attorney General of Israel, trial of Eichmann, District Court of Jerusalem, Criminal Case No. 40/61, mimeographed transcript, June 23, 1961, session 78, pp. Z1, Aa1, Bb1; June 26, 1961, session 79, p. B3; July 24, 1961, session 107, pp. E1, F1, G1.

105. Karl Wolff to Albert Ganzenmüller, August 13, 1942, Nuremberg trials document NO-2207. Asked about his choice of words, Wolff explained that the letter had been drafted by a young assistant. Interrogation of Wolff, February 5, 1962, Prosecutorial Staff of Landgericht Munich II, 10a Js 39/60, Protocol A, p. 23.

106. Report by a noncommissioned officer (Bergmayer?) of Secret Field Police Group 621, March 27, 1944, National Archives, Record Group 242, T 314, Roll 1458.

107. Walter Manoschek, ed., *"Es gibt nur eines für das Judentum: Vernichtung"* (Hamburg, 1995). This small book contains somewhat over 100 excerpts from almost 80 letter writers. The original collection of about 50,000

Now and then someone would employ or invent names for Jewish persons or for ghetto streets to make Germans laugh. The Interior Ministry's name expert, Hans Globke, drew up a list of first names for newborn Jewish children, featuring "Feibisch," "Schlämche," and the like.[108] Stadthauptmann Hans Drechsel of Kielce prepared a list for renaming streets in the ghetto, including Mojschegasse, Maselgasse (Good Luck Street), Ziongasse, Feingenblattgasse (Figleaf Street), Ritualgasse, Schamesgasse (Temple Keeper Street), Koschergasse, Trefegasse (Nonkosher Street), and, of course, Knoblauchgasse (Garlic Street).[109]

In private Jewish sources one may find simple words for Germans, like "murderers," "criminals," "sadists," and "beasts." Among eastern European Jews, a faceless perpetrator comes to the fore: he is the *malach ha-mavet*, the angel of death.[110] In later survivor accounts, however, such expressions disappeared.

Unusual is a juxtaposition of words or ideas, usually the hallmark of wit. Official correspondence left virtually no room

letters, compiled by Reinhold Sterz, is in the Bibliothek für Zeitgeschichte, Stuttgart. On garlic, see also Himmler to Pohl, May 27, 1944, Nuremberg trials document NO-30. On "frech," see also Oberstaatsanwalt (superior prosecutor) in Stolp, reporting on December 21, 1937, that a party official instigated 150 Germans to hound a Jew on such grounds. Gürtner diary, National Archives, Record Group 238, M 978, Roll 3.

108. Decree of August 18, 1938, *Ministerialblatt des Reichs- und Preussischen Ministerium des Inneren*, 1938, p. 1346.

109. The complete list, with the Polish and German names, is in Philipp Friedman, *Roads to Extinction* (New York, 1980), p. 75. Drechsel entered three possible German names for each street.

110. See the testimony of Rivka Yossalveska, Eichmann trial transcript, May 8, 1961, session 30, pp. L1-N1. Also, Elie Wiesel, "The Death Train" and Shmerke Kaczerginski, "The Girl in Soldier's Boots," in Jacob Glatstein, Israel Knox, and Samuel Margoshes, eds., *Anthology of Holocaust Literature* (Philadelphia, 1969), pp. 3-10, 291-298. The segment by Wiesel is translated from the original Yiddish text of his Auschwitz memoir.

for this literary form, but it does appear occasionally in private letters and testimony. A German soldier who passed through a Jewish quarter noted in a letter that the "aroma" (*Duft*) was "Mosaic,"[111] and a Jewish emigrant in the United States said, "When we had to leave Germany, we lost everything except the German accent."[112]

On the other hand, playing with words was an irresistible pursuit among many people in many locations. It was primarily an oral form of communication easily spread and remembered. Frequently critical of authority, it was also mildly subversive. When it was recapitulated in documents or testimony, its infectious nature lent a shimmering quality to a text. Here are a few examples.

A postwar German prosecutor, drawing up an indictment, wrote that in the labor camp Lipowa, near Lublin, the defendant Wolfgang Mohwinkel, an SS officer, had privately been called "Mordwinkel" by the inmates.[113] *Mord* means "murder" in German. At the end of 1940, when the German overseer of the city of Warsaw was Ludwig Leist, someone in the Jewish community, making use of the meaning of the German verb *leisten* (achieve) and mocking the chairman of the council, Adam Czerniaków, coined the phrase *Gott leistet Czerniakow* (God achieves Czerniakow).[114] The chairman, who heard of the saying, noted it in his diary.

The Security Police in Galicia quoted almost with relish the wordplays circulating in the area. Since the German name

---

111. Manoschek, *"Es gibt nur eines,"* p. 25.

112. Interview of Herbert Fromm in Geisel and Broder, *Premiere und Pogrom*, pp. 236–237.

113. Indictment of Wolfgang Mohwinkel in a Hamburg court, January 28, 1972, 147 Js 32/70.

114. Hilberg, Staron, and Kermisz, eds., *Warsaw Diary of Adam Czerniakow*, entry of October 1, 1940, p. 203.

for France was *Frankreich* and the name of the Generalgouverneur, who ruled Galicia and four other districts in Poland,
was Frank, his domain was called *Frank-Reich*. Slightly more
complicated was the talk about trustees. These men are called
Treuhänder in German, literally those with "loyal hands." A
German proverb is *Eine Hand wäscht die andere* ("One hand
washes the other"). The trustees who administered Jewish
property were often suspected of insider trading, and this
thought was expressed in the sentence, *Eine Treuhand wäscht
die andere.*[115]

During World War I, the highest German medal was the
Pour le mérite. In 1941 a highly educated letter writer on the
staff of XVII Corps in occupied Serbia referred to the Jewish
star worn on the front and back of clothing as the *Pour le
sémite.*[116] Although there is an implication of derision in this
rhyming, the meaning depends much on the context. When
the same expression was overheard on the stock exchange in
the occupied Netherlands, the German Security Police inter-
preted the joke as an attempt "to ridicule the identification of
the Jews."[117]

In irony the intended meaning of a statement is contrary to
its usual sense. If one follows this dictionary definition strictly,
examples are not abundant. Relatively simple forms, which
like wordplay are mostly oral in origin, were overheard and
preserved in testimony. More complex written commentary
appears mainly in personal diaries and memoirs.

A primitive inversion was used by an SS officer in Tre-

115. Kommandeur of Security Police in Galicia/III to Reich Security
Main Office/III A and D, National Archives, Record Group 242, T 175,
Roll 575.
116. Manoschek, *"Es gibt nur eines,"* p. 48.
117. Security Police Report No. 86 from the Netherlands, April 24,
1942, National Archives, Record Group 242, T 175, Roll 670.

blinka who trained his dog Barry (Barri) to attack and bite Jewish inmates severely. He called the dog "man" (*Mensch*) and the targeted victim "dog." He would then urge on the animal with the words "Man, grab the dog" (*Mensch, fasst den Hund*).[118] Somewhat more advanced was the idea of Alois Brunner, a deportation expert in Vienna, who is reported to have called himself *Jud Süss* (Jew Süss).[119] The original Jud Süss, popularly called, was Joseph Süss, or more fully Joseph Ben Issacher Süsskind Oppenheimer, who was a young man in the 1730s with wide power in the direction of financial affairs under the Duke of Württemberg. After the duke's death he was accused of crimes, including embezzlement, and hanged. His body was displayed in a public cage. Two hundred years later, in 1940, an anti-Semitic film with fictional components, *Jud Süss*, was released in Nazi Germany, where it was a considerable success.[120] Brunner, taken with the story, was obviously aware of the double allusion in the title. *Süss* means "sweet" in German.

Among Jews, irony was established practice, and it did not disappear in their hour of destruction. Dutch Jews awaiting deportation are said to have called their transit camp Westerbork-les-Baines (Westerbork Spa).[121] Among Orthodox Jews,

---

118. Adalbert Rückerl, *NS-Vernichtungslager* (Munich, 1972), pp. 188, 234–239. An SS man in Tarnów, Karl Oppermann, insisted that a Jew call his dog "Herr Rolf." Judgment against Oppermann, Landgericht Bochum, July 10, 1969, 16 Ks 1/68.

119. Statement by Anton Brunner (a Gestapo civilian employee), October 3, 1945, Dokumentationsarchiv des österreichischen Widerstandes, Vienna, Document 19061/2.

120. In the film, Süss rapes a young German woman who then commits suicide. The plot, with its anti-Jewish contents, was revived in a postwar version in a play by Rainer Werner Fassbinder, "Der Müll, die Stadt und der Tod," *Stücke 3* (Frankfurt am Main, 1976), pp. 91–128.

121. Jacob Presser, *The Destruction of the Dutch Jews* (New York, 1969), p. 438.

it is the custom to prepare the body of a deceased reverentially for burial by a communal fraternal society, the *hevra kaddisha*. In the death camp Treblinka, inmates gave the informal name *hevra kaddisha* to a Jewish Kommando which helped the Germans in conducting newly arrived Jews to the gas chambers, from where their bodies were dragged out for burning.[122]

Irony could be more fully developed in retrospective accounts and private journals. Eichmann in Israeli captivity wrote down his reminiscences. Describing his early days in the Security Main Office of the SS, he mentioned his supervisors. The first of them had talked incessantly. "Deaf he was, and when he talked he bent his powerful head backward so much that his beard was parallel to the ceiling and the floor." His next chief was an enthusiast about coins and medals. When Eichmann was invited by Leopold Itz Edler von Mildenstein to join a new section dealing with Jews, he gladly seized the opportunity to be rid of the "museum director." Portraying Mildenstein, Eichmann wrote:

> He was an Austrian, born somewhere in a corner of Moravia in the old Austro-Hungarian monarchy, by training an engineer. A man lacking in any military bearing who spoke evenly in a low sympathetic voice in a flow of even tones for whatever he had to say and who busied himself almost the whole day with graphic representations of the development of international Jewry in an organizational sense, the development of the Zionist world organization, the assimilationist direction of Jewry insofar as this could be recognized in any kind of little groups at all, and other similar drawings. Some of those sketched on cardboard

---

122. Yitzhak Arad, *Belzec, Sobibor, Treblinka* (Bloomington, Ind., 1987), p. 213. Arad cites a statement by Treblinka survivor Oscar Strawczinski, Yad Vashem Archives 03/3131.

were already hanging on the wall, some were still being worked on to complete the wall decoration.

A draftsman with missing teeth named Paul Demann, who was an older SS corporal from the Brandenburg area if I remember right, then drew up Mildenstein's concepts in a fine clear manner. . . . Everyone was clearly happy when the unending eight hours in the office were over.[123]

Eichmann, of course, was to head the Jewish section at the time of the Final Solution. Charts of deportation statistics were kept by his deputy, Sturmbannführer (SS Major) Rolf Günther. They were posted on the back of Günther's desk.[124]

The Warsaw ghetto, the largest in Europe, had a high death rate, but on the eve of the deportations, on July 22, 1942, its population was still close to 380,000. Six weeks later the roundups had not ceased and two-thirds of the people were gone. Rumors surfaced in the shrinking Jewish community that Britain would declare all the remaining Jews of Poland citizens of Palestine, that Polish Jews would be exchanged for Christian civilians living in the United States and Britain, and that Roosevelt would hold Germans residing in America as hostages to assure the safety of the Polish Jews. Hillel Seidman, the librarian of the ghetto archives, who was by profession a journalist, recorded the spread of these reports in his diary and went on to summarize a discussion in his office on September 2, 1942.

Dr. Yizchak Schipper [*sic*], the confirmed optimist, first began to examine the declarations from a legal standpoint

123. Eichmann's memoir written in Israel prison, *Die Welt*, August 17, 1999, p. 5.
124. Testimony by Eichmann, Eichmann trial transcript, session 94, July 12, 1961, p. Ee1.

(bearing in mind that he holds a doctorate in law) and comes to the inevitable conclusion that these announcements are perfectly feasible in international law.

Then he considers the political implications (after all he was also a parliamentary member of the Polish Sejm) and once again concludes that it is not only politically possible but even very likely. After that he begins to look for historical precedents (he is also an eminent historian), and then finally he examines the affair from the background of a seasoned activist (not forgetting his position as president of the Polish Zionist Federation), and proves that Jewish leaders in the West never sit back quietly or rest; they would storm the heavens in both America and England, and he quotes various names: Weitzman [*sic*], Ben Gurion, Greenbaum [*sic*], Harold Laski, Bernard Baruch, Morgenthau, and Herbert Samuel. They must have aroused the world's conscience and this is undoubtedly the result: these declarations we have all just heard about. The news must be 100 per cent accurate. . . .

Internally I feel stirrings of my journalistic training, urging me to uncover the prime source of all these stories, as well as the precise details (I am an archivist, too). . . .[125]

And this is the portrait of a pessimist, Josef Hertz, who headed the 6th Precinct of the Jewish police in the Warsaw

---

125. Seidman, *Warsaw Ghetto Diaries*, pp. 93–95. In Polish the historian was Ignacy Schiper. Chaim Weitzmann was the president of the World Zionist Organization; David Ben-Gurion headed the Jewish Agency in Palestine; Yizhak Gruenbaum was a member of the Jewish Agency Executive; the political scientist Laski taught in the London School of Economics; the financier Baruch was an adviser to Roosevelt; Henry Morgenthau was the U.S. Secretary of the Treasury; Samuel was a former High Commissioner of Palestine.

ghetto. The author is Stanislaw Adler, an officer in the head-quarters of the police in 1941.

> Josef Hertz of Region VI had a mental illness that I am unable to classify. A medium-tall, dark-haired man, with a short-clipped mustache, he received before the war the well-deserved nickname "Satan." Although he hated Hitler's Germans enormously, he believed very deeply in their victory. It was a point of honour with him to convince everyone that Hitler's defeat was an unattainable illusion and that every one of us locked into the ghetto was inevitably condemned to death. He would laugh merrily, rubbing his hands with ecstasy when his opponents could not refute his arguments and became inclined to admit that Hertz's reasoning was correct. While we all strove to keep ourselves above ground, thanks perhaps to some rationalization or some underground optimism, Hertz was quite properly assigned to Region VI which included the Jewish Cemetery.

Adler wrote his memoir while in hiding after the deportations. He survived but shot himself in 1946.[126]

126. Stanislaw Adler, *In the Warsaw Ghetto* (Jerusalem, 1982), p. 75. On his fate, see the introduction by Ludmila Zeldowitz on p. xvii.

FOUR

Content

◩ Every time an individual, organization, date, place, or event appears in the records, it becomes a potential building block for the researcher. These elements are deemed substantive and—unlike the formulaic or stylistic features of a document or statement—they may be found in various guides and indexes.

For the purposes of this chapter, however, the material will not be described under such headings as names, time frames, geographic areas, or notable occurrences. The most basic attributes of the contents lie somewhat deeper than these signposts, and to explore the bedrock one must ultimately look at items across the entire spectrum of the written sources and ask what was said there, or not said, in the first place. The initial query will therefore be devoted to premises on which the writing of that time was based. The next section will deal with kinds of information. Then the focus will be on omissions, followed by the problem of falsity.

PREMISES

In a broad sense, premises determine the boundary of a discussion. They may be assumed, requiring no explication, or articulated, to remove uncertainty and doubt. Either way they restrict the scope of propositions and arguments. This basic delimitation applies also to Holocaust sources.

Within the ranks of the perpetrators, the one premise that shaped all the orders, letters, and reports from 1933 to 1945 was the maxim that the Jews must be removed from German spheres of life. One could confer about the methods and pace of anti-Jewish actions, but objections had to be grounded solely in tactical considerations. Unquestioned and unargued, all manner of measures were simply a given, underscored with the single, frequently used word "selbstverständlich"—self-evident.

Not only was this idea the paramount premise in official German discourse, but even the need for its affirmation in meetings and correspondence was relatively rare. In a few instances a ranking official, expressing unease about some development, felt constrained to introduce his thoughts with a word about his continuing adherence to Nazi principle. In October 1941, for example, the Gouverneur of the Warsaw district, Ludwig Fischer, who was sufficiently disconcerted by the extraordinary death rate in the Warsaw ghetto to request higher rations "for the maintenance of Jewish productivity," raised that issue only after reiterating the reasons for Germany's "struggle with Jewry" and—with references to the ghetto population—the justification for directing "annihilating" blows at "this breeding herd from which world Jewry constantly renews itself."[1] More crisp, in November of that year, was Propaganda Minister Goebbels when he noted right

---

1. Summary, with verbatim remarks, of a meeting under the chairmanship of Generalgouverneur Frank, October 14–16, 1941, in Frank Diary,

after major deportations from the Reich had begun that the fate of the Jews, "although hard," was "more than deserved."[2]

The a priori acceptance of German policy was taken as a requirement by the victims themselves in preparing correspondence to the German administrative apparatus. Their reports and appeals to the Germans had to be in the German language, both literally and figuratively. Petitions had to incorporate German definitions, classifications, and assumptions as the basis for any argument. One could possibly invoke the "benevolence" of the German masters but not the ultimate question of right or wrong. Examples of this Jewish pleading are numerous.

Some small Jewish groups claimed that "racially" they were not Jews. An old Jewish sect known as Karaites, a community in the Crimea characterized as Krimchaks, and isolated Caucasian mountain Jews, the Tati, made such presentations. Only the Karaites succeeded.[3]

In several places where impressment for harsh labor was common, certificates of exemption became all-important as a means to claim immunity. When a Jew in Lvov was seized in 1941, he tried to explain that he had been arrested by mistake. The guard was unimpressed. "Yes, yes," he replied, "all the others are here by mistake too."[4] Sometimes, appeals empha-

National Archives, Record Group 238, T 992, Roll 5. Fischer's request was not granted.

2. Joseph Goebbels, "Die Juden sind schuld!" *Das Reich*, November 16, 1941.

3. On Karaites, see Dr. Steiniger, "Die Karaimen," *Deutsche Zeitung im Ostland* (Riga), November 15, 1942, p. 1., and correspondence in YIVO Institute document Occ Eba–100. On Krimchaks, see Reich Security Main Office IV-A-1, Operational Report USSR, No. 150, January 2, 1942, Nuremberg trials document NO-2934, and No. 190, April 8, 1942, NO-3359. On Tati, see Feldkommandantur Eupatoria to Army Rear Area 553 (11th Army), March 16, 1942, Nuremberg trials document NOKW-1851.

4. David Kahane, *Lvov Ghetto Diary* (Amherst, Mass., 1990), p. 35. Kahane's text is not a diary but a memoir he began writing while in hiding. See

sized Germany's best interests. In a typical plea for food, the chairman of the Jewish council in Pinsk wrote that Jewish men and women were "laboring in various enterprises, workshops, and factories for the need and to the large benefit of German offices," but that they had received, "besides bread, almost no other foodstuffs."[5]

So ingrained was the automatic incorporation of these ground rules that they could even appear in arguments *among* Jews. In the Romanian-administered Transnistrian ghetto of Djurin, a power struggle was waged between Jewish deportees from Southern Bukovina and those from areas that Romania had been forced to cede to the USSR in 1940. When the Romanians reoccupied their lost territory in 1941, they accused its Jewish inhabitants of having sided with the Soviets. The South Bukovina Jews in the Djurin ghetto, who had never been under Soviet rule, now claimed that they had been deported "unjustly."[6]

In Latvia, where Gypsies were concentrated, a twenty-one-year-old captive, Janis Petrovs, addressed a German potentate on November 21, 1941. He wrote in the name of all the Gypsies who had been crowded into the camps at Ludza, Rezekne, and Vilani. The Gypsy community was less experienced than the Jews in the fine art of petitioning. Petrovs asked such questions as: "Why were innocent women and children arrested? If they were really guilty of a crime, the place for them was prison." But Petrovs, like his Jewish coun-

---

also the attempt by Elchanan Elkes, chairman of the Jewish Council in Kaunas, to save Jews selected in "error." Avraham Tory, *Surviving the Holocaust— The Kovno Ghetto Diary* (Cambridge, Mass., 1990), p. 57.

5. Chairman of the Jewish Council in Pinsk to the German agricultural chief of the Pinsk area, January 21, 1942, Brest Litovsk Oblast Archives, Fond 2120, Opis 1, Folder 22, in Yad Vashem Microfilm M 41/881.

6. Wolf Rosenstock, "Die Chronik von Dschurin," entry of February 3, 1942, in *Dachauer Hefte 5—Die vergessenen Lager* (Munich, 1989, 1944), p. 50.

terparts, knew that he had to link his plea to a German interest. Winter was arriving, he said, and the Gypsies were working without pay, unable to buy anything. Their food consisted
of bad potatoes and seven ounces of bread a day. He asked the
Germans to set them free, but added, "or at least improve
their situation." The local Gebietskommissar, who read the
letter, wrote to the Generalkommissar of Latvia on February
26, 1942, explaining that the 234 inmates kept at Ludza were
the "asocial" elements of the local Gypsy population and that
the Security Police had "dissolved" the camp at the end of December.[7]

The "at least" in the Gypsy plaint, which is reflected also
in Jewish appeals, was lodged in the minds of the victims from
the beginning, and it was voiced as the situation worsened in
the vain hope that new lows would not become even lower.
That which had already happened was, on the other hand, no
longer a subject of much discussion. The process, as spokes-
men for the victims learned very quickly, was not reversible.

In the German hierarchy the precept that actions against
Jews were necessary did not have to be reiterated, but the nature of this process and the methods of its implementation
called for subsidiary premises that were articulated again and
again. In the main these were disciplinary requirements to ensure the purity of German motives, such as the rule that all
measures against Jews were an undertaking of the Reich for
the welfare of the German people, and not an opportunity for
private enrichment. From this principle flowed the insistence,
enshrined in a decree, that firms pay a tax for having acquired
Jewish companies at prices below market value.[8] For Himmler
it was selbstverständlich that SS men deliver everything taken
from Jews to the Reich, and that transgressors would be dealt

7. The correspondence is in the German Federal Archives, R 92/522.
8. Decree of December 3, 1938, RGBl I, 1709.

with severely.[9] Not tolerated either, at least theoretically, was any behavior that appeared to satisfy a base instinct. Although this prohibition was seldom enforced, one finds it in pieces of paper that had to be signed by the Auschwitz guards to the effect that only the Führer had the power to make decisions about the life or death of an "enemy of the state" and that the individual SS man was not allowed to harm an inmate "bodily."[10]

The axiom that Jewry could not be a part of Germandom gave rise to a number of corollary propositions that addressed the consequences of apartness. One was the inference that a variety of internal Jewish institutions could be left undisturbed. The Reich Citizenship Law was the first major occasion for such a pronouncement when it prohibited Jews from displaying the swastika banner but expressly permitted them to hoist the blue-white-blue Zionist flag.[11] Of course, Jewish organizations were reluctant to avail themselves of this right in very public places, lest such an act be deemed provocative in Nazi eyes, but their flag did have "legal protection." Analogous to the division of flags was the handling of cultural events. Germans were not supposed to perform Jewish music, and Jews were not to play compositions by Germans. This conceptualization was applied in Germany and later in the Netherlands, the ghetto of Theresienstadt, the Warsaw ghetto, and elsewhere.[12] In the domain of law, the Jewish community of Berlin was allowed to adjudicate disputes between

9. Himmler's speech to SS-Gruppenführer meeting in Poznań, October 3, 1943, Nuremberg trials document PS-1919.

10. See United States Holocaust Memorial Museum Archives, Record Group 04 (Główna Komisja Badania Zbrodni Hitlerowskich w Polsce), Roll 2 (Auschwitz Archives).

11. Law of September 15, 1935, RGBl I, 146.

12. Geisel and Broder, *Premiere und Pogrom.* Adler, *Theresienstadt*, pp. 584–623. Isaiah Trunk, *Judenrat* (New York, 1972), pp. 215–229.

Jews before a Jewish arbitration tribunal,[13] and subsequently the practice was extended to ghettos in Poland and Lithuania.[14]

A doctrine of noninterference was also set forth in matters of procreation and child protection. A court in Celle exonerated a Jewish woman who had sought an abortion, on the ground that the law was designed only for the welfare of the German people.[15] A few years later an exemption from the abortion law was weighed analogously for Polish women.[16] Since Poles were also an increasingly segregated population, the Law for the Protection of German Blood and Honor of 1935, which prohibited Germans and persons of "related blood" from having sexual relations or entering into a marriage with Jews, was formally decreed in 1941 *not* to apply to such intercourse or unions between Poles and Jews.[17] By the same token, Polish laborers in Germany were risking their lives if they touched a German woman,[18] and in large parts of the incorporated territory they were prohibited—coincidentally on the same day as the issuance of the 1941 decree—from

13. Note by Werner Best on behalf of Himmler to Justice Minister Gürtner, March 17, 1938, as summarized in the Gürtner Diary, National Archives, Record Group 238, M 978, Roll 3.

14. Trunk, *Judenrat*, pp. 180–184. Note also the criminal jurisdiction of the Jewish ghetto authorities in Łódź, in Dobroszycki, *Chronicle of the Łódź Ghetto*, entries of April 8, 1941, December 2, 1941, and December 16, 1941, pp. 44, 87–88, 95. Historically this exemption may be traced to Roman late antiquity. See Michael Maass, ed., *Readings in Late Antiquity* (New York, 2000), p. 194.

15. Note by a prosecutor in Celle, November 20, 1938, as summarized in the Gürtner Diary, November 22, 1938, National Archives, Record Group 238, M 978, Roll 3.

16. Reich Chancellery memorandum of March 27, 1941, Nuremberg trials document NG-844. The conferees considered this liberalization for Polish territories incorporated into the Reich.

17. Decree for the implementation of the Law for the Protection of German Blood and Honor, March 31, 1941, RGBl I, 297. The removal of the prohibition did not extend to those Poles who became naturalized or those who were inscribed in a newly created list of ethnic Germans.

18. Ulrich Herbert, *Fremdarbeiter* (Berlin, 1984), pp. 127–129.

marrying Germans or ethnic Germans.[19] Their position in German eyes was consequently clear beyond doubt. Why, then, the measure that seemed to grant them a license with respect to Jews? In fact, Poles had never contemplated intimacies with Jews before the war. In Germany, Polish workers were rarely assigned to cities, where the Jews lived, and within the incorporated territory Poles and Jews had already been partitioned de facto, particularly where ghettos were established. The decree, which awarded the Poles an ostensible freedom, was therefore not written to expand their opportunities. It was, however, crafted to complete a logical thought. When prohibitions, like the Blood and Honor Law, are deemed beneficial, and a particular population is to be excluded from the benefit, that group receives a liberty.

In line with this exclusionary thinking, Poles could also be held to a lower standard than Germans. In one instance, a German potentate in Poland could see no reason for harshness in the case of a Polish woman who had killed her four-day-old child in 1941. She was married, but her husband had been a prisoner of war since 1939, and the father of the child was another man. The woman's mother pleaded for mercy, and the *Kreiskommissar* of Grodno reacted magnanimously:

In reply to your appeal of December 19, 1941, with reference to the arrest of your daughter for infanticide, I state that in the German Reich one thinks differently about crimes against life. Nevertheless, I have taken into consideration the special circumstances to order the release of your daughter on March 31, 1942.[20]

19. Majer, *"Fremdvölkische,"* pp. 433–434. The prohibition was a secret Erlass by Gauleiter Greiser.

20. Michalina Janulewicz to Landrat of Grodno, December 19, 1941, and Kreiskommissar of the Grodno district to Mrs. Janulewicz, January 19, 1942, United States Holocaust Memorial Museum Archives, Record Group 53.004 (State Archives of Grodno Oblast), Roll 1, Fond 1, Opis 1, Folder 2.

At the time of the Final Solution, when all the Jews, including Jewish children, were to be killed, temporary exceptions had to be made for irreplaceable "useful" laborers retained in construction and industry. These people happened to be young, healthy adults, some of whom also possessed special skills. Left alive, they would have the strength to survive all the road building despite little clothing, shelter, and food. In the end they might even become the nucleus of a new, stronger Jewish community. That postulate of natural selection was raised to the status of a premise when it was unambiguously expressed by Heydrich in the Final Solution conference of January 20, 1942. It was the lesson of history, he said, that survivors of heavy labor were the toughest element, and they would therefore have to be "dealt with appropriately."[21]

But if the possibility of a resistant remainder was a danger sign for Heydrich, it was also a slender hope of some Jews during this lethal period. Viktor Frankl was a fit man, physician, poet, caricaturist, mountain climber, and—later in life—licensed pilot. Frankl, who survived Auschwitz, leaned on Friedrich Nietzsche, one of whose dicta he made his own: "What does not destroy me makes me stronger" (*Was mich nicht umbringt macht mich stärker*).[22] And this was an entry of an adolescent girl in her diary:

Be brave! Let us remain aware of our task and not grumble, a solution will come. God has never deserted our people. Right through the ages there have been Jews, through all the ages they had to suffer, but it has made them strong,

21. Summary of Final Solution conference of January 20, 1942, Nuremberg trials document NG-2586.
22. Viktor Frankl, *From Death Camp to Existentialism* (Boston, 1992), p. 89.

too; the weak will fall, but the strong will remain and never go under.[23]

KINDS OF INFORMATION

The information in the sources may be characterized in three ways. (1) It may be general or detailed. (2) It may be positive, based on explicit passages, or negative, when it is deduced from the absence of any notation or remark. (3) It may be firsthand or reprocessed. These attributes may be turned into questions: How much and what kind of detail can be found? Which conceivable occurrences can be negated because they are not mentioned? And what is the nature of second- or thirdhand materials?

Generality and detail may be distinguished most easily in circulating documents. Here the boundaries of the correspondence are generally set by their level. Since the major administrative structures are triangular, the laws and commands issued at the apex are the most embracive and therefore the most general. The highest officials not only state what must be done, they also delegate authority, allowing the middle-level administrators to spell out the task to lower-ranking subordinates. Instructions consequently become more elaborate in the course of the descent to the bottom of the administrative hierarchy. Reports, in turn, reflect the greatest specificity when they are composed on the lowest rung of the ladder. They will then be combined and distilled by higher-ranking recipients for presentations to the chiefs.

The reason why central authorities must leave discre-

23. Anne Frank, *The Diary of a Young Girl* (Garden City, N.Y., 1967), entry of April 11, 1944, p. 228. She died in Bergen-Belsen a few weeks before the liberation of the camp.

tionary space to lower decision-makers is the impossibility of covering every detail and contingency in a single central enactment. One of the most tightly constructed decrees, which dealt with a relatively simple subject, was the measure signed by Heydrich and dated September 1, 1941, requiring the Jews to wear the star in public. In six short paragraphs the decree provided for the size, color, and placement of the patch, its nonapplicability to Jews in privileged mixed marriages, the penalty for infractions, and its territorial extent to the Reich and Bohemia-Moravia.[24] Yet a number of matters were not included: the production and distribution of the stars, the payment for them, how they were to be sewn on clothing, the question of whether they had to be worn by Jews working in segregated groups indoors or by Jews of specified foreign nationalities. Also left to additional instructions was the introduction of the yellow star in the incorporated territory of Silesia seized from Poland, where a blue star had already been decreed.[25] The marking of Jews in occupied territories, as in the Netherlands or the Generalgouvernement in Poland, or in satellite states, is a parallel but separate story with its own details. There one encounters not only differences of design, such as armbands in the ghettos of Poland and buttons in Bulgaria, but also different histories, including decisions to rescind the measure in Romania and Bulgaria when those two countries recoiled from maintaining the star as a stepping-stone to mass deportations.

Confiscatory measures were more complex. In the Reich the November 12, 1938, decree imposing a billion-mark

24. RGBl I, 547.
25. For Upper Silesia, see the order of the directorate of the Jewish "Interest Representation" (*Interessenvertretung*) in Będzin, September 20, 1941, United States Holocaust Memorial Museum Archives, Record Group 15.060 (Żydowski Instytut Historyczny), Roll 1 (Collection Będzin).

"fine" on the Jews had just two operative paragraphs with a total of thirty-three words,[26] but implementation decrees and guidelines were needed to specify who would have to pay the fine, the schedule of payments, the acceptance of securities and other assets in lieu of cash, the deductibility of amounts paid from another tax, and so forth. Again, on the eve of deportations, when impoverished Jewish communities were deprived of their apartments and personal belongings save for a limited number of enumerated items that could be taken along, the details were the subject of lengthy directives.[27] The process did not stop after the Jews had already vanished. Under the 11th Ordinance to the Reich Citizenship Law, dated November 25, 1941, the property of Jews who had left Germany was subject to seizure. The remaining items included not only real estate and bank accounts but the value of life insurance policies and contractual pensions. The pensions were to be handed over to the Reich in lump sum, and that procedure generated an extensive correspondence. Some of the former employers of deported Jewish pensioners complained that the demand for payment was excessive, and an arbitration tribunal then settled these disputes, taking into account "all circumstances" and a "humanly possible" calculation of the life expectancy of each individual. In a concession, the arbitrator ruled that if a Jew died "unexpectedly early," a rebate could be requested. Additional complications, however, could arise when, for example, the holder of a pension and his wife committed suicide right after they had received a notice

26. RGBl I, 1579.
27. See the Finance Ministry directive (signed Schlüter) of November 7, 1941, Nuremberg document NG-5784. For Luxembourg, see United States Holocaust Memorial Museum Archives, Accession No. 1999 A 0015, Rolls 1 and 2. For the Netherlands, see the facsimile of a Security Police order in Herbert Boucher, *Miracle of Survival* (Berkeley, Calif., 1997), pp. 125ff.

of "evacuation to east." Inasmuch as the couple had not physically crossed the border, did not the obligation to continue payments cease forthwith? No, was the answer of the Gestapo, because the notice signified that the death (*Ableben*) occurred after the commencement (*Eröffnung*) of the evacuation.[28]

Detail automatically increased when orders were issued to implement an action in the field. After the bulk of the 2nd Lithuanian Police Battalion was assigned in October 1941 to the German 11th Reserve Police Battalion to carry out mass shootings in Byelorussia, the Lithuanian commander issued a departure order containing the names of 487 Lithuanian officers and men.[29] At the local level, the subject of an order could be very small and its contents very detailed. Thus a German police president in Upper Silesia ordered the Jewish council in Będzin, known there as the "Jewish Interest Representation" (*Jüdische Interessenvertretung*), to make the following announcement about Jewish pedestrian traffic:

> More than before, the Jewish population has to take care that it yields in a timely manner sufficient space on sidewalks to uniformed members of German offices or posts and to Germans recognizable by the insignia they wear. This is to be communicated to the Jewish population.
>
> Furthermore, the Jewish population is to be made aware of the following: When Jews walk along a street that

28. The 11th Ordinance is in RGBl I, 722. On bank pensions, see the file of the Private Bank Association, National Archives, Record Group 242, T 83, Roll 97. On arbitration, see the letter of the Deutsche Länderbank, Berlin, March 31, 1942, and for the case of the double suicide, the Legal Division of the Commerzbank to the Private Banking Association, June 18, 1942, *ibid.*

29. Order by Major Antanas Impulevicius, Commander of the 2nd Lithuanian Police Battalion, October 6, 1941, Lithuanian State Archives, Fond 1444, Opis 1, Folder 3.

is barred to them [*Judenbannstrasse*] to go to an office or when they have to perform an occupational task there, and they walk on a Judenbannstrasse for such purposes based on the required certificate, then that has to be done on the shortest route: the Judenbannstrasse has to be entered and exited through the nearest streets that are generally open to Jews.

Anyone contravening this order has to expect severe measures by the police.[30]

In a local situation, precise instructions would sometimes be drawn up for a single operation like a shooting. In November 1941 the Byelorussian town of Slutsk had been the scene of a riotous roundup by the 11th German Police Battalion and its Lithuanian companies. At the start of 1943 a remnant ghetto still existed there. To avoid any repetition of the 1941 experience, the ghetto's final destruction was planned minutely. On February 5, 1943, the Kommandeur of Security Police in White Russia, Obersturmbannführer (SS Colonel) Eduard Strauch, issued a four-page order for the action, which was to take place on the 8th and 9th. German personnel were directed by name to their posts, and a Latvian Security Police company of 110 men in the service of the Germans was also posted. At the shooting site, called "resettlement grounds" (*Umsiedlungsgelände*), there already were two pits. At each of them two groups of SS officers and men of the Security Police were to be stationed, so that one group could replace the other every two hours. Security at the site was to be provided

30. Announcement by the chairman of the Jewish Interest Representation of Będzin, September 1, 1941, incorporating the order of the Police President in Sosnowiec, dated August 23, 1941. Underlining in text. United States Holocaust Memorial Museum Archives, Record Group 15.060 (Żydowski Instytut Historyczny), Roll 1 (Collection Będzin).

by another detachment, transport from the ghetto by yet another, and supplies of ammunition by two more SS men. During the action, members of the Order Police were to be posted at the ghetto while six Kommandos led by Germans and manned by Latvians were assigned to the task of "bringing up" (*Aufbringung*) the Jews. Six trucks were to be assembled, and four Latvians were to guard the Jews on each vehicle. Yet another German officer was to be responsible for the food rations and quarters of the participating force.[31] Every detail in this order was spelled out so that the plan could be carried out meticulously.

Special conditions in a locality might similarly call for particular specifications. The area commissar (Gebietskommissar) of the rural region near Vilnius (Wilna-Land), Horst Wulff, ordered the fencing of the "places of Jewish liquidation" (*Plätze der Judenliquidation*). Then he demanded that lime be strewn into the "liquidation" sites and that they be covered with earth.[32] Finally he wanted to have details about their size and location. From Trakai came the answer that there were four graves in that small subdistrict alone: one measuring 80 by 4 by 4 meters, another 33 meters long, and the two others 30 meters long.[33]

If one may view the communications of Wilna-Land Gebietskommissar Wulff as the last link in a chain of orders, the information from Trakai is on the ground level. That is where

31. Order by Strauch, February 5, 1943, United States Holocaust Memorial Museum Archives, Record Group 53.002 (Belarus Central Archives), Roll 6, Fond 845, Opis 1, Folder 206.

32. Excerpts of the correspondence, dated February and April 1942, in Benz, Kwiet, and Matthäus, eds., *Einsatz im "Reichskommissariat Ostland,"* pp. 80–81.

33. Main Lithuanian Health Service in Trakai to Kreiskommissar Wilna-Land, July 8, 1942, Lithuanian State Archives, Fond 613, Opis 1, Folder 10.

the greatest detail is found in the reporting structure. Often this detail contains the names of individual persons. After Kharkov fell into German hands, the local municipality had to register the city's population. In that city, bound volumes were produced in which the names were arranged according to street address, and Jewish residents appear in the registry, segregated on yellow pages.[34] In Będzin the Jewish council made an alphabetical list of all the community's 22,174 people.[35] In monthly mortality reports of the Lublin ghetto, sequences of names were determined by date of death.[36] In Luxembourg and France, names were typed on deportations lists.[37]

On occasion a local name list affords an insight into the character of an operation. Such a document is a report of a roundup of Jews in the Galician city of Lvov (Lviv in Ukrainian) by Ukrainian police. The names are those of Ukrainian policemen, and the report is a part of a series—so routine was this kind of activity in the summer of 1942.[38]

34. See Kharkov Oblast Archives, Fond 2982, Opis 6. Also in the archives is a placard containing instructions of the Ukrainian city administration for registration. Persons registered were required to show their Soviet internal passports, which indicated the holder's nationality. In the passports, Jews were a nationality separate from Ukrainian, Russian, etc.

35. United States Holocaust Memorial Museum Archives, Record Group 15.060 (Żydowski Instytut Historyczny), Roll 2 (Collection Będzin). The list is not dated.

36. See the reports for November 1941 and January 1942 in United States Holocaust Memorial Museum Archives, Accession No. 1998 A 235 (Archiwum Państwowe w Lublinie), Roll 1.

37. On Luxembourg, see United States Holocaust Memorial Museum Archives, Accession No. 1997 A 0080. On France, see Serge Klarsfeld, *Memorial to the Jews Deported from France 1942–1944* (New York, 1983), pp. xvii–xx.

38. A facsimile of the original Ukrainian-language document is in Michael Hanusiak, *Lest We Forget* (New York, 1975), p. 92, and a translation is on p. 93. The name Lehmann is corrected and the information in the brackets is added here. Hanusiak included a few dozen items from Commissariats I to VI. The documents are in the Lvov Oblast Archives.

Lviv, August 22, 1942

5th Commissariat of
Ukrainian Police in Lviv
No. 2826/42

Subject: Jewish action carried out on August 21, 1942
Reference: Order of Ukrainian Police Commandant

To Commandant of Ukrainian Police in Lviv

I hereby report that on August 21, 1942, 805 Jews were delivered to the assembly point from the 5th Ukrainian Police Commissariat area.

Revolver shots fired		
1/ Viytovich, Mikhailo fired		1 shot
2/ Zherebukh, Andriy "		1 "
3/ Krivistky, Lev "		2 "
4/ Petruschevksy, Lev "		2 "
5/ Kalimum, Ivan "		2 "
6/ Borukh, Roman "		4 "
7/ Fitjo "		4 "
8/ Leskiv, Mykola "		4 "
9/ Stakhiv, Timko "		6 "

Total shots fired   26
Killed 12 Jews, wounded 3

A total of 1,095 zlotys were taken from the Jews as bribes, and at the direction of [Lieutenant] Lehmann [German Order Police] are enclosed herewith.

Enclosures: 2

Head of Commissariat

In transmissions to higher echelons, names are turned into numbers, bullets may become a volume of ammunition, and the enterprises, housing, or personal belongings taken in the course of confiscatory operations are combined into Jewish assets no longer connected to their individual owners.[39]

Quantity of detail is reflected not only in the levels of orders and reports. It is also correlated with the bureaucratic layers in which conference records and letters were produced. The conferences were meetings between persons of equal rank or between representatives of organizations with equal standing in a forum. Copies of summaries were distributed in the first instance to participants. In deliberations at the top, the issues were larger than in discussions on a middle or lower plane, and that distinction is mirrored in the recapitulations of what was said. Letters were by definition exchanges between equals, and in these instruments the scope of a subject, regardless of the opinions expressed, depended primarily on the position of the writers in the bureaucracy.

Conferences had agendas. Typically they lasted an hour or two, and their constraints limited asides and elaborations. The summary, which was a version of what was expressed, could and often enough would incorporate not only the subject at hand but also the interests and purposes of the preparer.[40] Like conferences, letters had a topic. They were not confined to any length, and they were the actual words of their authors,

39. For a summation of Jewish losses, see the reports of SS statistician Korherr to Himmler, covering the period to the end of 1942, and for some areas through March 1943, in Nuremberg trials document NO-5194. A partial summary of confiscations is in a report by the remnant administration (*Restverwaltung*) of the Finance Ministry to the Allied Control Commission, November 14, 1946, Nuremberg trials document NG-4906.

40. A stenographic record of the Final Solution conference of January 20, 1942, was made, but it has not been found. The summary, written by Eichmann at the direction of Heydrich, went through several drafts. See Eichmann's testimony at his trial in Jerusalem, June 23, 1961, session 78, English transcript, pp. Aa1, Bb1; June 26, session 79, pp. A1, F1; and July 24, 1961, session 107, pp. E1, F1, G1. The specific reference to a stenographer is in session 107, p. F1.

but at the very least the writers of this correspondence observed custom and ritual in the choice of their words. Generally letter writing was prompted by a need, such as reliance on an organization for information or help, or by an emerging conflict.

In a typical request, a noncommissioned officer of the Ethnic German Relief Agency (Volksdeutsche Mittelstelle) wrote to the gendarmerie post in Jaworów for a donation of furniture and old clothes from "secured Jewish things" to a Ukrainian woman whose son had been killed while fighting in the SS in Russia.[41] A roofing company wrote to the SS Central Construction Office in Auschwitz about its difficulties in obtaining raw material for a project in the camp.[42] A Gestapo man in Vienna wrote a letter of recommendation for an employee whose accomplishment it was to have emptied out the apartments of 48,500 deported Viennese Jews in record time.[43] And so on.

Less plentiful but on a higher tier was the correspondence generated by interagency strains. The unprecedented actions against the Jews and the concomitant growth of bureaucratic free will created situations in which one organization found itself in a contest with another. In Łódź, for example, a struggle ensued over the uses of Jewish property confiscated in the

41. The letter, dated November 18, 1942, is in the United States Holocaust Memorial Museum Archives, Accession No. 1995 A 1086 (Lvov Oblast Archives), Roll 1, Fond 11, Opis 1, Folder 48. A number of such requests are included in this roll.

42. VEDAG (Vereinigte Dachpappenfabrik Betriebe, Schlesien, in Breslau) to SS Central Construction Directorate (Zentralbauleitung) in Auschwitz, June 26, 1942, United States Holocaust Memorial Museum Archives, Record Group 11.001 (Center for Preservation of Historical Documentary Collections, Moscow), Roll 41, Fond 502, Opis 1, Folder 307.

43. Karl Ebner to office of *Reichsstatthalter* in Niederdonau, praising Bernhard Witke, July 5, 1943, Dokumentationsarchiv des österreichischen Widerstandes, Folder 8919/6.

ghetto,[44] and in the Generalgouvernement the German railroads were on a collision course with the SS over the retention of a sizable Jewish labor force during the deportations.[45]

In all the material circulating through the channels of administrative machinery, the contents down to the smallest detail were selected or prescribed for specific, identifiable objectives, and within that context every item of information was meant to be functional. Such limits did not apply to private diaries, memoirs, or proffered testimony. There the choice of facts was not governed by a rule book. Any subject and any episode might therefore emerge. Generally, however, one may distinguish between two kinds of facts in these accounts, one that will illuminate the author's surroundings, the other in which the author is also the subject.

Scattered in the compendium of survivor accounts are flickers of sights that had been glimpsed in a single minute. A Jewish labor official in the Łódź ghetto observed the arrival of Czech Jews at the railway station in the fall of 1941 and overheard someone ask, "Where can we get a taxi? Is there a hotel?"[46] A woman from eastern Poland remembered that her father, an intellectual who had always been a fastidious dresser,

44. See the letter of the chief of the Main Trusteeship Office East, Max Winkler, to Finance Minister Lutz Schwerin von Krosigk, December 20, 1940, Zentralarchiv (Central Archives of the German Democratic Republic) Potsdam, Collection 21.01 (Reichsfinanzministerium), B 6159, and subsequent correspondence in the folder.

45. Adolf Gerteis (President of the Ostbahn) to Higher SS and Police Leader Friedrich Wilhelm Krüger of the Generalgouvernement, September 16, 1942, and to the Transport Ministry on the same date, Zentralarchiv Potsdam Collection 43.01 (Reichsverkehrsministerium), Laufende Nummer neu 3128.

46. Interview of Bert Fleming, May 16, 1996, United States Holocaust Memorial Museum Archives, Record Group 50.030*0365. In Łódź, Fleming's name was Bernhard Fuchs.

was led away in his shirtsleeves.[47] Another woman noticed during a roll call in Auschwitz that the body of a baby had been washed into the ditches.[48] Incidents like these, which were indelible in the minds of the witnesses, are least likely to be recounted in official sources.

An individual who remained in a particular place for an extended time could sometimes spot the odd effects of unceasing deprivation. Stanislaw Adler, the Jewish police lieutenant in the Warsaw ghetto, noticed that well-to-do Jews paid high rates for a respite in the Jewish mental hospital at Otwock.[49] Elie Cohen, a physician deported from the Netherlands, found indications that the frequency of several common diseases, including hives, asthma, influenza, gastric and duodenal ulcers, eczema, and hypertension, tended to *diminish* among the inmates of Auschwitz, and that the symptoms of diabetics were also reduced.[50]

On occasion someone who was at the right place at the right time could fill a gap in the documentary evidence. Eichmann recalled in Argentina that he was the one who composed the three paragraphs that Heydrich submitted to Göring on July 31, 1941, and that became, with Göring's signature, an empowerment that enabled Heydrich to organize the "final solution."[51] Villagers living in Bełżec, who were drafted to perform work in the construction of the death camp nearby, were able to date the start of that crucial project.[52]

---

47. Interview of Charlene Schiff, March 23, 1993, *ibid.*, *0203.
48. Interview of Ruth Meyerowitz, February 20, 1990, *ibid.*, *0161.
49. Adler, *In the Warsaw Ghetto*, p. 108.
50. Elie Cohen, *Human Behavior in the Concentration Camp* (New York, 1953), pp. 63–65.
51. Eichmann, *Ich*, p. 479.
52. Statements by Eustachy Ukrainski, October 11, 1945, and Stanislaw Koyak, October 14, 1945, in Oberhauser (Bełżec) case, Landgericht München I, 1 Js 278/60, VI, 1117–1120, 1129–1133.

Any number of accounts are centered not so much on an environment as on the self. This category of the literature contains little uniformity, but at the opposite ends of the range one may identify two variants. There are action stories, filled with dramatic incidents, one after the other, without stops for frequent or long reflection, and there is introspective writing in which thoughts and afterthoughts are put forward distinctly.

Reproducing a chain of experiences that followed one another in rapid succession is typically the stuff of an escape story. A member of a Hungarian labor company who worked himself out of a grave, where he had been left for dead, recapitulated the encounters he had on the way to safety.[53] A Viennese, repeatedly caught, described how he was finally loaded onto a train headed for Auschwitz and how he jumped out of the moving transport.[54] A Gypsy who deserted from a German army unit in Poland wrote about fleeing to the Soviets, who almost shot him as an enemy when the German invasion began, and about his timely liberation by the advancing German army, which almost condemned him to death for his desertion but then released him because he was unworthy of being a German soldier in the first place.[55]

The fortunes of these people were rare, and hence their narratives are unusual. Generally these texts contain at least a hint of triumph, even a cause for celebration. Quite different is the situation of a person who had a much more common experience but one which was a galling personal defeat, or bit-

53. "The Memoirs of Zalman Teichmann," ed. Nathan Eck, in *Yad Vashem Studies*, vol. II, 1958, pp. 261–294. The original manuscript is in Yiddish.

54. Leo Bretholz (with Michael Olesker), *Leap into Darkness* (Baltimore, 1999).

55. Alfred Lessing, *Mein Leben im Versteck* (Düsseldorf, 1993).

terly frustrating helplessness, or the realization of having done something catastrophic. Such incidents might not have been communicated so readily, and to the extent that the words were committed to paper, their primary medium was some form of diary.

The Generalgouverneur in Poland, Hans Frank, kept a diary that was an official log of his speeches, cultural events in his residence, travel itineraries, minutes of conferences he chaired, and reports he received. In 1942, however, he inserted two personal statements in this record. Both were signed by him but not addressed to anyone. The first, dictated as a "protocol" and dated August 28, 1942, is eighteen typewritten pages long. The opening paragraph is the climactic one. Frank had tendered his resignation to Hitler. He explained this decision by noting that Hitler had removed him from his concurrent post as head of the German Academy of Law and had forbidden him to make public speeches. The Führer had lost confidence in him. Frank attributed this development to the police. Germany, said Frank, had become an arbitrary police state that denied elementary rights to Germans, whereas he had always believed in security under law and the idea of freedom. That view, he insisted, had nothing in common with liberalism, parliamentary government, decadence, or Judaism. It stemmed from old Germanic custom. Now the Gestapo and the authoritarianism of the police were ascendant, and his enemies were continually at work to undermine him. Frank was thinking of leaving to join his family that very night.

In the second statement, which is undated, Frank noted that Hitler had rejected his offer to resign. Referring to the serious situation at the front, Frank affirmed that he would remain at his post even though the inroads into his power in the Generalgouvernement were continuing. It was clear to him, he said, that the complete destruction of security under law by means of the concentration camp and police arbitrariness constituted the gravest danger to Reich and Führer, but he was fated to be an observer unable to alter events, even while his enemies in their "blind hatred" sought to "eliminate" him.[56]

Frank, an early Nazi, had played a major role in the subjugation of the Poles and the annihilation of the Jews. As late as August 15, 1942, he had made a speech to Nazi party officials in the Generalgouvernement asserting that "compassion" (*Mitleid*) with the Jews would be "misplaced." By the end of the year he was losing his battle for power with Himmler, but to the end he never abandoned his Nazi faith. Only at his trial in Nuremberg did he proclaim a guilt that would not be erased in a thousand years.[57]

Some Jewish diaries reveal the intense reactions of their authors in Dostoevskian scenes. Two illustrations may be drawn from private notes kept in ghettos during the summer deportations of 1942. At that juncture, Jewish councils in Poland mobilized their resources and personnel in the service of the Germans, hoping that a controlled operation would be a limited one and that a core of the Jewish population would be allowed to continue its ghetto existence. in Łódź, Jewish physicians, including several who had arrived the year before from Bohemia-Moravia, determined which people were not fit enough to stay. A teenager in the ghetto, Dawid Sierakowiak, wrote in his diary that his mother had fallen victim to the "bloodthirsty German Nazi beast," and "totally innocently," he added, "because of the evil hearts of two Czech

56. National Archives, Record Group 238, T 992, Roll 6.

57. Speech of August 15, 1942, Frank Diary, Nuremberg trials document PS-2233. Testimony by Frank, April 18, 1946, International Military Tribunal, *Trial of the Major War Criminals*, XII, 13.

Jews, the doctors who came to examine us." A seventy-year-old neighbor, who was an uncle of the ghetto's chief doctor, "had been left untouched," he went on, "and my healthy (though emaciated) mother had been taken in his place." The "shabby old doctor" had searched and searched but could find no disease in her. "Nevertheless, he kept shaking his head, saying to his comrade in Czech: 'very weak, very weak.'" Then the diarist wrote the following paragraph:

> After the doctors announced the verdict, and Mom, unfortunate Mom! was running like mad around the house, begging the doctors to spare her life, Father was eating soup that had been left on the stove by the relatives hiding in our apartment, and he was taking sugar out of their bag! True, he was kind of confused, questioned the policemen and doctors, but he didn't run out anywhere in the city; he didn't go to any friends' connections to ask for protection. In a word, he was glad to be rid of his wife with whom life had become harder and harder, thus pushing Mom into her grave.[58]

In the ghetto of Otwock, near Warsaw, Calel Perechodnik was a member of the Jewish police. He wrote about his experiences retrospectively with passages placed under specific dates to give part of the text the appearance of a diary. What he said there with chagrin and despair is unsurpassed in any contemporary account.

In 1942, Perechodnik was twenty-six years old. He had a wife, Anka, and a daughter, Aluśka, whose second birthday was

---

58. Alan Adelson, ed., *The Diary of David Sierakowiak* (New York, 1996), entry of September 5, 1942, pp. 208–226. Sierakowiak died in the ghetto. His diary was translated from the Polish by Konrad Turowski. The translation was edited.

August 19. That morning the ghetto was surrounded. "Satan," he said, laughed when he saw "how 'smart' Jews are unwittingly helping the Germans, how they are saving them work." The Jewish police were told to herd the ghetto's inhabitants to the public square with a promise that their own families would be freed. The policemen ran "as if possessed," blowing whistles without pause. Anka, afraid, hid in the cellar. After the chief of the Jewish police reassured Perechodnik about the release of the policemen's wives and children, Anka went to the square, but she became suspicious when the chief's wife was not there. She concluded that only those who had hidden would live. "No, no, no," Perechodnik answered. As shots rang out, the Jews were told to sit in the hot noonday sun. A friend of Perechodnik's, also a policeman, took off his armband and quietly joined his wife, "an honorable man." Poles passed by in trolleycars, looking out at the Jews. After some time, Anka wanted her husband to obtain some poison for her and the child. Perechodnik asked a Pole to go to the pharmacy, but the Pole returned shortly, saying he needed a prescription. A Jewish doctor in the square handed Perechodnik the piece of paper through the barbed wire. When Anka was about to swallow the Luminal, her sister knocked the glass of water out of her hand. Finally the selection was made after all. The policemen retrieved their wives and children from the crowd and loaded the mass of people onto the cattle cars, but after the boarding, the Germans began to separate the policemen from their families. Through the din, Anka called out to him, "Calek, Calek, what am I to do?" Perechodnik rushed to the child, and placed her off to the side. "She stands alone, hungry, sleepy, surprised. Maybe she does not understand why her father, always so good to her, leaves her in the dark. She stands alone and does not cry." Suddenly the Germans ordered the policemen to march fast to the other side of the square. From the distance in the night, Perechodnik could see only clouds of dust and silhouettes. "God, have mercy on me." After his escape, he lived until October 1944.[59]

Most of what is known, in large measure or small, comes directly from the sources in the form of data and descriptions. But what if one looks for confirmation that something did or did not happen, only to find silence in the materials? When that point is reached, the blank may signify not nonexistent information but information about a nonexistence.[60] Here are a few examples of such conclusions.

The outstanding illustration is the absence of a written order by Adolf Hitler to annihilate the Jews of Europe. Oral instructions by Hitler to carry out the Final Solution were cited by Himmler, and specific demands by Hitler with respect to Hungary or Slovakia appear in the records, but neither a plenary command with Hitler's signature to kill the Jews, nor any reference to such a document, has ever been found. It is not as though Hitler had never communicated fundamental decisions in writing. He had issued a brief order that brought about the euthanasia program affecting mental patients and he had signed a directive to launch the invasion of the USSR, but in the case of the Jews he evidently did not dictate anything to be preserved on a piece of paper. Many implications flow from this negative fact, be it about the supreme sensitivity of the issue, a period of hesitation, an evolving crys-

59. Calel Perechodnik, *Am I a Murderer?* (Boulder, Colo., 1996), trans. and ed. by Frank Fox. Perechodnik died in Warsaw before the arrival of the Red Army. The original text is in Polish. The title is taken from a line in the diary. The episode of August 19, 1942, is on pp. 32–51. Calek is a Polish diminutive of Calel.

60. In historiography this method is more common than might be supposed. Louis H. Feldmann, in his *Jews and Gentiles in the Ancient World* (Princeton, 1993), p. 193, refers to the weakness of the *argumentum ex silentio*, but uses it extensively himself.

tallization, or a mode of binding together leaders and enforcers in an act of historical proportions.

More frequent than an uncertainty about a pivotal turning point are questions about the incidence of specific occurrences. In essence, one might wish to know how many times, or to what degree, something might have happened. If an answer is not found in a summary, the search must encompass a significant number of sequential reports. Suppose that the inquiry is centered on the resistance of the Jews in the course of the mass shootings by the Einsatzgruppen during 1941 and 1942, and that some numerical assessment is sought by adding the numbers of Einsatzgruppen men lost in these operations. Scanning the nearly two hundred daily consolidated reports prepared in Berlin, one discovers no mention of any Germans killed by Jews.

Detail is salient. If it is out of context, its meaning and significance may not be apparent, but it is always recognizable. Silence is less obvious. One must be aware of it before it yields its information. Hearsay may or may not be evident; in texts it is signaled as such only when there is an attribution. References to prior sources, however, may be made in two ways: either a particular person or organization is named, or else an unnamed individual or amorphous group is indicated.

An example of a complete citation is a dispatch of August 27, 1942, by Ambassador Abetz in Paris, who reported a conversation with French Premier Pierre Laval, in which Laval had talked about a letter by the Archbishop of Toulouse to priests in the diocese calling upon them to protest from their pulpits in the strongest language against the deportation of the Jews.[61] That month the French collaborationist govern-

---

61. Abetz to Foreign Office, August 28, 1942, Nuremberg trials document NG-4578.

ment in Vichy had begun to hand over foreign and stateless Jews from the unoccupied zone of France to the Germans. To the churches the French premier had declared that he would brook no interference; in conversations with the Germans he was at pains to point out his specific difficulties with the clergy.

On the other hand, Jews who kept diaries in ghettos were sometimes especially careful when they wrote about matters that came to their attention, lest their notes fall into German hands and implicate a neighbor or acquaintance. In one Warsaw ghetto diary, ten printed pages covering four dated entries contain passages with following phraseology:

> "I met a girl there aged around 19 or 20 who arrived today. . . . The girl gave me an appalling account . . ."
>
> "I . . . met a Jew with whom I had been acquainted before the war. . . . In the short conversation I had with him he laid bare before me . . ."
>
> "I ran into another acquaintance who told me . . ."
>
> "A woman acquaintance of mine told me the true story. . . ."
>
> "The same woman told me about two other events. . . ."
>
> "The news was brought by a woman who fled to Warsaw. . . ."
>
> "Two Jews told me today . . ."
>
> "Refugees from Aleksandrów Kujawski told me a few days ago . . ."
>
> "One of my closest friends told me . . ."
>
> "Yesterday I heard . . ."
>
> "Word has it . . ."
>
> "It is said . . ."
>
> "This is the story as I heard it. . . ."

"I have heard the details . . ."
"Today a Jew who generally has accurate information
told me . . ."[62]

When a rumor, referring to an event, is mentioned in reports or diaries, one must keep in mind that the event may or
may not have transpired as told, and that it could even have
been invented whole. But the rumor in itself is always a fact.

On April 8, 1942, a Pole who lived in the vicinity of the
newly established death camp of Bełżec noted in his diary that
every day one train left from the city of Lublin and another
from Lvov, each with about twenty cars, for Bełżec. There the
Jews got off, went behind a barbed-wire fence, and were
killed, so far as he had heard with electric current or poison
gas. Along the way, he wrote, people—notably railway men—
saw horrible things.[63] Remarkable in this entry is its date,
which shows how quickly the news was spreading barely two
and a half weeks after the opening of the camp. Even the
method of killing, which was out of sight, had been narrowed
to two possibilities, one of them true.

Five months later, also in the Lublin district, a German
army officer was reported to have passed a rumor to a judge
that many Germans in the United States were shot in reprisal

62. Abraham Lewin, *A Cup of Tears*, ed. Antony Polonsky (Oxford,
1989), pp. 61–70. The diary, unearthed in Warsaw, is not complete. See also
Tory's *Kovno Ghetto Diary*, which contains material that the author had
added to the original manuscript after the war. The supplementary information came from other former ghetto residents. Editor's footnotes on pp. 5,
11, 59. The additions to passages, however, are not specifically identified, so
that original observations and hearsay are not separated.

63. Diary of Zygmunt Klukowski, *Dziennik z lat ocupacji Zamojszyzny
1939–1944* (Lublin, 1959), pp. 251–254, partially translated into German in
Peter Longerich, ed., *Die Ermordung der europäischen Juden 1941–1945* (Munich, 1989), p. 198.

for the treatment of the Polish Jews.[64] The rumor was base-
less, but it confirms an awareness of the Jewish fate and reveals
a German thought about America.

What if the author of a report made no reference to the
origin of incorporated material? If a signatory presented a numerical compilation without disclosing where the figures
came from, the interpretation of the document may be difficult. One must realize, for example, that the SS statistician
Korherr wrote down totals of Jewish dead without including a
tabulation of the 363,211 Jews shot by the Higher SS and Police Leader South, Hans-Adolf Prützmann.[65] Similarly, some
background is needed to interpret the draft report of Einsatzgruppe A, replete with the map showing numbers in caskets,
because no footnote is furnished to make clear that the toll
claimed for Latvia includes more than 27,000 Jews shot in
Riga by the Higher SS and Police Leader North, Friedrich
Jeckeln, with little or no help from the Einsatzgruppe.[66]

The situation becomes more opaque when an eyewitness
fails to acknowledge the inclusion of hearsay in an account.
Unlike some functionary in a bureaucratic agency, the author
is presumed to have observed matters directly, unless another
source is cited or intimated in the testimony. The user may, of
course, suspect a problem, but if no doubt arises, the deriva-
tive nature of the contents will not be recognized. Moreover
the extent of this borrowing across the whole of accumulated
testimony is for all practical purposes unknowable.

64. Main Division Propaganda of the Generalgouvernement, consolidated weekly reports from district propaganda divisions in September, report of the Lublin division, September 5, 1942, YIVO Institute document
Occ E 2-2.
65. The Korherr report with amendments is in Nuremberg trials documents NO-5194 and NO-5193. Prützmann's report, December 26, 1942, in
National Archives, Record Group 242, T 175, Roll 124.
66. Draft report, ca. January 31, 1941–February 1, 1942, Nuremberg
trials document PS-2273.

OMISSIONS

The Polish poet and essayist Jaroslaw Rymkiewicz became interested in the geography of a Warsaw square, known as the *Umschlagplatz* during the occupation, which was actually a railhead at the border of the ghetto, surrounded by buildings. It was a facility for freight shipments until the time of the deportations, when more than 300,000 Jews were transported from there to Treblinka. Rymkiewicz could not find photographs or other visual descriptions detailed enough to satisfy his curiosity about the size and configuration of the surrounding buildings that stood there at the time, and the adjacent walls, gates, and sentry boxes. He needed that information because he pursued questions about the reactions of the Jews held in the so-called *Durchgangslager* (Dulag, or transit camp), which was their enclosure pending transport, and about the awareness and feelings of any Polish onlookers. He wondered about the possibilities of escape as well as those of rescue. Since he could not read Hebrew or Yiddish, he consulted several dozen accounts in the Polish language, but these sources said "next to nothing" about the physical layout of the place.[67]

A pertinent fact left out of a source is an omission. The particular point of concern to a researcher may not have been included because an author saw no need to do so. Alternatively it might have been excluded on purpose.

In correspondence and diaries, an entire range of subject elements is omitted as a matter of course. Whoever writes to someone is usually aware that the intended recipient already has certain facts. What is verbalized consists only of an increment—the new information added to the old. A researcher,

---

67. Jaroslaw M. Rymkiewicz, *The Final Station: Umschlagplatz* (New York, 1994), particularly pp. 46ff.

however, is not the addressee and may not have the necessary background knowledge to understand the document completely. Details will therefore float in the text as unanchored fragments. This state of affairs is even more characteristic of a diary.

Even the smallest omissions may be troublesome. The European habit of using only last names is a veritable invitation to confusion. It is common to be confronted with a Müller in a file when there were three or four Müllers in the same organization. The diary of Adam Czerniaków, who headed the Jewish council in Warsaw, contains approximately three hundred names. In these pages there could have been a father and a son, two brothers, two namesakes, or simply one person with the same name as another who does not appear in the diary at all.

Conversations on the telephone or in person, which form the antecedents of a correspondence, might turn up there only in a cryptic reference. A notation in the appointment calendar of Heinrich Himmler, dated December 4, 1941, reads: "9:30 p.m. SS-Obergruppenführer Jeckeln Jewish question."[68] Jeckeln was the Higher SS and Police Leader in Riga. Five days earlier he had carried out a massacre of the ghetto's Latvian Jews, and three days later he conducted a second massacre just as Jews began arriving from Germany. What, precisely, had Himmler said to Jeckeln?

When recollections are offered on tape, in print, or un-

68. The conversation took place in Hitler's headquarters after dinner. Other ranking SS officers were present at the dinner table, but the two men may have been alone when the Jewish question was discussed. How much time was devoted to the topic is also unclear. Himmler indicates that the SS brigades and SS economic enterprises were also mentioned. The entry is in Himmler's own Germanic-script handwriting. Calendar, in Center for Preservation of Historical Documentary Collections, Moscow, Fond 1372, Opis 5, Folder 23.

published to an archives, the witness makes a judgment of what may be of interest. Generally the discarded facts comprise very ordinary things. In the case of survivors, coverage is often spotty with regard to prewar experiences, such as the extent of one's education; the family's income, savings, and possessions; the size of an apartment; the availability of amenities, including sewerage or running water; the state of one's health; attitudes toward immediate family members; and all the other factors that determine initial conditions and capabilities. Even when life in a ghetto is described, the nature of constrictions, particularly in monetary terms, are not always spelled out, nor are tensions with persons in close proximity. The survivor wants to come to the point, which is principally an experience radically different from that of the audience.

Much is simply not remembered. The Auschwitz commander, Rudolf Höss, mentioned a conversation with Himmler about the Final Solution in Berlin but had manifest difficulties with a reliable date or month of the meeting. Eichmann was able to describe exactly how Heydrich had told him about Hitler's order for the physical annihilation of the Jews, but he could not recall the week, month, or season when he was given that news. Similarly, many survivors do not list the date of their deportation. Chunks of past events fall away inexorably in the minds of perpetrators and victims. The phenomenon in general is familiar enough. In a painting by Salvador Dali it is represented by wilting watches and bullets in the air fired by unseen shooters. On the X-Y axis of a social scientist, the decay is charted in a concave curve. Primo Levi wrote forty years after the liberation that the remaining witnesses "have ever more blurred and stylized memories."[69]

Paired with something no longer remembered is a memory

69. Primo Levi, *The Drowned and the Saved* (New York, 1986), p. 19.

that cannot be expressed. This is a common inability.[70] How does one describe the utter deprivation of possessions and privacy in a camp, the filth, the smell, the exhausting labor and endless roll calls, the cold, the heat, the persistent hunger, the thirst, the confrontation with the sudden loss of a wife, a husband, a child, the momentary fear of being gassed, the constant anxiety interrupted only by deep sleep? David Olère was not a writer but a skilled painter who lived in France. He was deported to Auschwitz in March 1943. There he was employed as an illustrator, but he also emptied gas chambers of corpses. After the war he recounted to his wife the things he had seen. When she could not believe him, he sketched or painted his recollections. In the sketches he drew cross sections of the gas chambers and cremation facilities with careful precision, but in most of the paintings he mixed—as though struggling with the reality—caricature, symbolism, and fantasy: the piglike face of an SS-man, a skull instead of a face under a helmet, and scenes of apotheosis.[71]

In sum, much is unsaid in routine correspondence and ordinary testimony. There may have been no necessity to mention or explain something, or no awareness of its possible significance to someone in the future, or no capacity to shape it in words or pictures. The circumstances are altogether different, however, when a fact is concealed by an author who fears exposure for transgressions, or who is reluctant to disclose weakness and humiliation.

Personal knowledge is hidden completely when a person is

70. See Harald Welzer, *Verweilen beim Grauen* (Tübingen, 1997), pp. 123ff.

71. David Olère, *The Eyes of a Witness*, with an introduction by Serge Klarsfeld (Paris, 1989). Olère, born in Poland, was over forty at the time of his Auschwitz experience.

in hiding. That was the case when the SS and Police Leader of Galicia, Fritz Katzmann, lived incognito in West Germany after the war. Somewhat more common was the behavior exemplified by Josef Löwenherz, former chairman of the Jewish council in Vienna, who maintained a public silence. Still others would fail to reveal in their testimony particular activities in which they had been involved. The former Reich Minister for War Production, Albert Speer, never alluded to his correspondence about Auschwitz and other matters that had been overlooked at Nuremberg. There were also those who would censor their volunteered accounts lest they reveal the one incident that would expose them to moral condemnation. Finally, some would hesitate to answer a question until prodded to do so, and a few would withhold facts and feelings for many years before disclosing them.

Carefully fashioned autobiographical statements are a feature of several entries in postwar yearbooks of the German Who's Who. In these volumes a reader would not learn that Max Bardroff of the Dresdner Bank was involved in Aryanizations of Jewish enterprises in the Netherlands, that Kurt Eisfeld of I. G. Farben served in a leading position of his company's chemical plant in Auschwitz, that Joseph Gebhardt of the Finance Ministry played a crucial role in the confiscation of the Ignatz Petschek coal mines, that Gebhardt's colleague in the ministry, Richard Kallenbach, corresponded about the costs of transporting Jews deported from France, that Erwin Massute of the German railways was in charge of operations in the network of the Generalgouvernement in Poland, where many transports originated and where they also arrived from distant points of departure, and that Friedrich Vialon of the Ministry of Eastern Occupied Territories was responsible for confiscations of the personal possessions of the

Baltic and Byelorussian Jews.[72] For others as well, whose am-
bitions had not abated after 1945 and who sought higher
office or commercial success in the Federal Republic of Germany, the decades of their continuing careers were not a time
to advertise their earlier exploits.

Germans were not the only ones to use caution. In com-
paring a published account of a survivor's life in the Łódź
ghetto with that author's typescript in the Jewish Historical
Institute in Warsaw, Robert Moses Shapiro found that references to the memoirist's service in the ghetto police had been
deleted.[73]

In interviews, some survivors faced a quandary when the
subject turned to something particularly painful and burden-
some. Abraham Bomba had been a Jewish barber in Treblinka
who cut off the hair of Jewish women about to be gassed. During the filming of *Shoah*, Claude Lanzmann wanted him to
give a precise description of what was happening when the
hair was cut. Did Bomba work with scissors? Was there a mirror? How many women in the room? How did Bomba feel?

"I can't. It's too horrible."
"We have to do it. You know it."
"I won't be able to do it."
"You have to do it. I know it's very hard. I know and I
apologize."
"Don't make me go on please."
"Please. We must go on."

72. For these entries, see the volumes of *Wer ist wer?* published in the
1950s and 1960s.
73. Robert Moses Shapiro, "Diaries and Memoirs of the Łódź Ghetto in
Yiddish," in Shapiro, ed., *Holocaust Chronicles* (New York, 1999), pp. 95–124,
particularly pp. 101–102, 113–114. The diary was written by Shlomo
(Szlama) Frenkel, who changed his name to Frank after the war.

And he went on, after one of the longest pauses in cinematic history.[74]

The hiatus was much longer in the case of Viktor Frankl, the Viennese psychiatrist who had survived Theresienstadt, Auschwitz, and a satellite camp of Dachau. His memoir, *Man's Search for Meaning*, written immediately after the war, had small sales at first, but eventually the number of copies may have reached nine or ten million in German and translations. The memoir was in many ways incisive and detailed, with mentions of Frankl's young wife who was deported with him and who did not survive. Yet a good deal was left unsaid. He was clearly a Jew, but on no page did he identify himself as such.

Frankl became a public figure, and forty years after the war he broke his reticence about details pertaining to his personal life. He was nearly ninety years old when a new short book of reminiscences he had written down over the years was published under the telling title *Was nicht in meinen Büchern steht* (What is not said in my books). There he talked about his mother, who was descended from the great eleventh-century rabbi Rashi, as well as the Prague sage Rabbi Löw, known as the "Maharal." Frankl described his father as a spartan and stoic man whose traits, he said, became his own. In Theresienstadt, where his father, eighty-one years old and half starved, wrestled for breath with terminal lung edema, Frankl gave him a lethal dose of morphine. He had married his first wife, a twenty-one-year-old nurse at the Jewish hospital, in 1941. She had an abortion, orally decreed for Jews in Vienna, and after their deportation from Theresienstadt to Auschwitz in October 1944, he never saw her again. Then he said something he had not related earlier for the simple reason that he was not

74. Claude Lanzmann, *Shoah* (New York, 1985), pp. 111–117.

sure it had actually happened. During the selection on his arrival in Auschwitz, two lines were formed. When he saw only
strangers in his line, he walked unseen by the SS to the one
where he had spotted younger colleagues. He had made the
right choice, avoiding the gas chamber. On a later occasion, a
"gangster" who had become a capo shoved an inmate with
blows and curses into a group of a hundred men and pulled
out Frankl. The hundred, Frankl believed, were either headed
for the gas or some destination bound up with extreme danger. For decades, he said, he never dreamed about the criti-
cally important examination, the *Matura*, which had to be
passed to enter the university, but always about Auschwitz, the
true test of his maturity.

After his return to Vienna he married another nurse, Elea-
nore Katharina Schwindt. Some people, he reported, wondered why he stayed. Had all that had been done to him and
his family been too little to persuade him to leave Austria? His
father had died in Theresienstadt, his mother had been gassed
in Auschwitz, his brother had also perished there, and his wife
had died at the age of twenty-four in Bergen-Belsen, but he
would reply: "What has anyone done to me?" (*Was hat mir wer
angetan?*).

Frankl's last book was published obscurely, not celebrated
anywhere. He died two years later in the city in which he was
born.[75]

Another physician, Elie A. Cohen, who was deported from
the Netherlands to Auschwitz, spent fifteen months in the

75. Viktor E. Frankl, *Was nicht in meinen Büchern steht* (Munich, 1995).
See also the obituary by Holcomb B. Noble in *New York Times*, September
4, 1997, p. D7. The approximate dating of his stays in Theresienstadt and
Auschwitz is deducible from the book. See also Adler, *Theresienstadt*, p. 735.
The ghetto museum of Theresienstadt could find no records of Frankl's ar-
rival and departure. Jan Munk, director, to author, April 6, 2000.

camp. A few years after the war he wrote a medical treatise, based largely on his own observations, about the physical and psychological condition of the prisoners as well as the attitudes of the SS. Cohen was not a diversified genius like Frankl but a discerning country doctor, and the tone of his book was clinical and dispassionate. He made no attempt to cover all his pre-Auschwitz experiences, especially those in the transit camp of Westerbork. Since he strove in his analysis to make generalizations, he included his own adaptations only as illustrations of what he regarded to be the common pattern of victim responses. He noted explicitly, for example, that he had heard about the gassing of Polish Jews as early as 1942, and that he "surely could not have pretended ignorance" of the gas chambers when he was on his way to Auschwitz, but he explains that no one knew that most Jews would be gassed on arrival. After he learned that his wife and child had been killed, he realized that he himself might shortly be dead. At this point he had an "acute fright reaction." His sole remaining thought was his own survival, and he was convinced that his only chance lay in "the medical field." With that aim in mind he sought a position as a physician in a prisoners' hospital. "The interests of my fellow prisoners I did not consider at all."[76]

But this was barely half the story. Twenty years later another book, based on interviews he gave, appeared. It was titled *The Abyss*, with the subtitle *A Confession by Elie A. Cohen*. Here he recounted his blunders in rejecting an opportunity to hide with his wife and child, in advising his sister not to hide, and in trusting someone who, for money, would arrange for stowaway places on a freighter carrying lumber, a commodity that was relatively scarce in Holland, to richly forested Swe-

---

76. Cohen, *Human Behavior in the Concentration Camp*, particularly pp. 119, 123–124.

den. In Westerbork, where he was working as a physician, he had power to designate people as unfit for transport because of a fever or other medical problem, and he did so also for some who were healthy until he was found out by the chief inmate doctor. Then he stopped. He "collaborated." Judging himself, he said, "that wasn't very nice of me; it wasn't decent, and it wasn't courageous. It is a fact, one of the facts, of which I am ashamed." When he arrived in Auschwitz he stood with his father-in-law, who was over seventy, when suddenly someone called out, "Doctors, step forward." He did so immediately. When he was told that his wife and little boy were no longer alive, he believed it right away. It did not come "entirely as a surprise," even though he had not imagined a situation in which arriving deportees would be gassed without delay. In the hospital hut a "lunatic" escaped in the middle of the night. When the man was found and returned, the inmate block doctor told Cohen to kill him lest six hundred people in the hospital be endangered. Cohen or another physician—he did not remember which of the two—gave the man two hundred units of insulin. The next time Cohen had "far fewer moral scruples," and "that man died as well."[77]

Another twenty years had passed when Cohen produced an essay titled "The Guilt of the Germans." He was eighty years old by that time, and this is what he had to say:

> My hatred of the German people is great, and it does not abate, since I never met a German who said to me: "I feel guilty for what we have done to the Jews." . . .
>
> Do I have guilt feelings? I don't feel guilty for having survived while so many were murdered. Among them were

77. Elie A. Cohen, *The Abyss* (New York, 1973), particularly pp. 59–66, 80–88. The original Dutch edition appeared several years earlier.

my wife and child. That Germans gassed them like mad dogs fills me with anger against the German people.

I feel guilty, however, since I worked for the Germans: In the transit camp of Westerbork I was a transport physician and in Auschwitz an inmate physician, and I assisted in selections to the gas chamber.

My own explanation is: I wanted to live and for that I did much. Today I find that I crossed the norms of humanity. But that is easily said.[78]

In their first autobiographical works, Frankl and Cohen used their own experiences as illustrations for a thesis, limiting what they said about themselves, obliterating much that affected them acutely, and channeling every one of their comments into an overall explanation about life in a drastic situation. In their delayed disclosures the hidden facts come to the fore. Here the two men show that they were capable of rapid self-preserving calculations, even of deliberate killing under circumstances thrust upon them as physicians. In old age they also displayed their postwar attitudes to the Germans. Their reactions were exact opposites in that Frankl all but exonerated his fellow Viennese, and Cohen condemned the German people totally. Yet on any conceivable scale both of these statements are extremes, and in contrast to the constraints placed on an intellectual exploration they are extremely personal.

78. Elie A. Cohen, "Die Schuld der Deutschen," in Helmut Schreier and Matthias Heyl, eds., *Das Echo des Holocaust* (Hamburg, 1992), pp. 19–25, on pp. 21, 22. The conversation took place earlier. Cohen was born in 1909.

FALSITY

The factual contents of sources are not always true in their entirety. Falsity is common enough to take a variety of forms, but once it is identified, it will usually fall into one of two categories. It will either be an inadvertent error or a willful misrepresentation.

The simplest of all errors pertain to a number or the spelling of a name. In some cases these mistakes are evident, as in a numerical addition that may be incorrect on its face.[79] Misspelled names are a recurrent feature, which can often be checked. Was the name of the Einsatzkommando leader in Byelorussia Vilbert or Filbert?[80] Was the commander of the 707th Division von Bechtholzheim or von Bechtolsheim?[81] Was the SS and Police Leader in Lublin Globotschnigg, Globocnic, or Globocnik? Himmler solved that problem by calling him "Globus," an affectionate contraction that conveyed the wide reach and considerable importance of that officer.[82] Since the German army also had generals with French and Polish names, eternal vigilance was required to avoid a

79. In Jäger's compilation of shooting operations by his Einsatzkommando, dated December 1, 1941, there are inaccurate additions for three locations: Alytus (August 13), Ukmerge (August 19), and Vilnius (September 12). See his report in Center for the Preservation of Historical Documentary Collections, Moscow, Fond 500, Opis 1, Folder 25.

80. He appears misspelled as Vilbert in the War Diary of the 403rd Division/Ic, June 30, 1941, National Archives, Record Group 242, T 315, Roll 2206.

81. It is Bechtolsheim, but misspelled in hand-lettered tables of organization for the units of the Commander of Rear Army Group Center, January and February 1942, *ibid.*, T 501, Roll 15.

82. See Himmler's handwritten entry in his appointment calendar, September 3, 1941, Center for the Preservation of Historical Documentary Collections, Moscow, Fond 1372, Opis 5, Folder 23. The correct spelling is Globocnik.

spelling mishap, and that challenge was not always mastered. In many diaries and memoirs, a witness who never saw a name in type could render it only phonetically. Additional complications would then arise in transliterations from one alphabet into another, notably the Latin, Cyrillic, and Hebrew.

Next to inaccuracies in numbers and names, there are hapless errors stemming from faulty observations and failing memory. Anything could be misremembered: the layout of a camp, the steps of an administrative procedure, or a person's features. Elie Wiesel's memoir *Night* has a description of a hanging watched by a crowd of inmates. In his account, which involves a trio, two men die on the ropes but a boy is still moving. A man near Wiesel asks, "Where is God?" and a voice "within" Wiesel answers that He is hanging on the gallows.[83] The depiction is Christological because Jesus on the cross was flanked by two other crucified men. Wiesel's boy, however, was in reality a grown man.[84]

In the case of the denaturalization of John Demjanjuk before a United States district court in Ohio, five surviving Jewish inmates of Treblinka testified against the defendant and misidentified him as "Ivan the Terrible," a nickname given by the prisoners to a Ukrainian guard who herded Jewish deportees into the gas chambers and activated the gassing. One witness said that the defendant had given him twenty lashes, another that a prisoner was tortured by Demjanjuk with a wood drill. Moreover, some of the survivors testified that from the fall of 1942 they had had repeated opportunities to ob-

83. Wiesel, *Night*, pp. 75–76.
84. Statement by Zygfryd Halbreich, October 17, 1973, through the courtesy of Mr. Halbreich. The names of the three hanged men, who had attempted an escape, are in the statement.

serve Demjanjuk in Treblinka.[85] Demjanjuk, however, who had been a guard in other camps, was not Ivan the Terrible. He only resembled him. After his extradition to Israel, where he was condemned to death, the mistake was finally proved at a hearing in the Israeli supreme court, and he was sent home to Ohio.[86]

In war crimes trials at Nuremberg, a member of the prosecutorial staff would question defendants or other witnesses at some length, and the gist of the answers would be cast into an affidavit to be signed, subject to corrections, by the deponent. As a result, the wording might not reflect what had actually been said. When the former Auschwitz commander Rudolf Höss was interrogated, he could have been dazed, no longer caring what would be attributed to him. In the affidavit that he signed on April 5, 1946, the casualty figure for this camp is three million—almost three times the actual toll, and one of the three death camps in the Generalgouvernement is misidentified as "Wolzek." In the same affidavit all three of these centers were falsely placed under the Security Police, and all are stated to have been in operation by June 1941, even though Bełżec did not begin until March 1942 and Sobibór until April of that year. Treblinka, which actually launched its operations in July 1942, is said to have "liquidated" eighty thousand Jews, principally from the Warsaw ghetto, in six months, when in fact the death toll during that time was in the hundreds of thousands.[87]

85. The judge ordered the denaturalization on the basis of this testimony. *United States v. Demjanjuk*, 518 F. Supp. 1362 (1981).

86. For Demjanjuk's return, see Yoram Sheftel, *Defending Ivan the Terrible* (Washington, D.C., 1996), pp. 407–445. Sheftel was one of his defense attorneys in Israel.

87. Affidavit by Höss, April 5, 1946, Nuremburg trials document PS-3868. Such misstatements do not appear in his subsequent testimony or in his autobiography.

When incorrectness is intentional, it may be contained in a denial or a fabrication. Denying a fact is reactive. It is a false answer deliberately given by someone who is on the defensive. A fabrication, on the other hand, is something made up to impress a readership or audience. Most of the time the fabricator is taking the initiative.

Among accused perpetrators, knowledge or complicity in matters pertaining to anti-Jewish actions was almost routinely denied. The former Staatssekretär of the Foreign Office, Ernst von Weizsäcker, testified in Nuremberg with respect to his signature on a document for the deportation of French Jews, that really he had had no jurisdiction. He had to sit at a desk, he said, and papers came across this desk.[88] Another ranking official, Ernst Kaltenbrunner, who took over the Reich Security Main Office in January 1943, asserted at his trial in Nuremberg that he was a figurehead, that the offices IV and V (Gestapo and Criminal Police) were directly under Himmler's control, and that he himself was ill informed about their activities.[89] Kaltenbrunner could make use of the fact that after Heydrich's assassination in June 1942 and before his own appointment, the vacancy had not been filled. He also knew that the Gestapo chief Heinrich Müller was missing, that Criminal Police chief Arthur Nebe had been purged in 1944, and that Müller's expert in Jewish affairs, Eichmann, had not been heard from. He could surmise that the prosecution did not have the correspondence in which he himself had urged Himmler to deport five thousand elderly Jews from There-

88. Testimony by Weizsäcker, Nuremberg subsequent trials, Case No. 11 (*United States v. Weizsäcker et al.*), English transcript, pp. 8569, 8581, 8590. Weizsäcker was convicted for his role in the deportation of Jews from France.

89. Testimony by Kaltenbrunner before the International Military Tribunal at Nuremberg, *Trial of the Major War Criminals* (Nuremburg, 1946–1948), XI, 237–246, 267.

sienstadt, that it had not discovered an order he had signed for the deportation of Jews who were former nationals of various countries, and that it did not have a copy of a letter Himmler had sent him requesting monthly statistical reports of Jews who had been shipped off.[90]

Denial was practiced also by much-lower-ranking individuals. Elmars Sprogis, who came to the United States after the war, had been assistant chief of police in the Latvian town of Gulbene in July 1941. In that capacity he had arranged for the transfer of nine arrested Jews to another town where they were to be shot with other Jews. A U.S. district court dismissed the government's suit to revoke his acquired American citizenship, and that judgment was affirmed by a federal circuit court, but in a concurring opinion one of the circuit court judges was bothered that Sprogis had initially denied any involvement in the processing of the nine Jews, including an order he had given that they be guarded and other acts respecting their confiscated personal property. Only when he was confronted by telltale documents signed by him did he change his story.[91]

A former member of a Lithuanian police battalion in German service, Jonas Bauzys, whose education was limited to four years of school and who exercised no command function at all, testified at a pretrial denaturalization hearing in the United States about his role. He had served in the Lithuanian army when that country was still independent before the war,

90. On Theresienstadt, see Kaltenbrunner to Himmler, February 1943, Himmler Files, Folder 126, Manuscript Division of the Library of Congress. Himmler did not approve that suggestion. On nationalities, see Kaltenbrunner's order of March 5, 1943, Nuremberg trials document NG-2652-A. On statistics request, see Himmler to Kaltenbrunner, April 9, 1943, Nuremberg trials document NO-5197. Kaltenbrunner was nevertheless convicted and hanged.

91. *United States v. Elmars Sprogis*, 763 F. 2d 115 (1985).

in the Lithuanian Territorial Corps under Soviet rule, and in the police battalion under the Germans. When his unit was sent to Italy, he deserted to the II Polish Corps fighting with the Allies. That particular trajectory, it should be noted, was not altogether unusual. When Bauzys was asked after the war by American officials whether he had been affiliated with any police formation, he answered in the negative. The 15th Battalion, of which he was a member, had participated in several actions against Soviet partisans, in the course of which thousands of Jews were killed. In the preliminary hearing of 1992, conducted by the U.S. Justice Department to explore the revocation of his American citizenship, Bauzys stated among other things the following:

> In Lithuania was not organized killing Jews or something. If some people did for revenge. You know. Individual people for revenge. You know. They did it. Okay. Not involved. You can kill me today. You can do anything with me. Not involved.

When the Justice Department attorney, Denise Slavin, said that the historian engaged by the department had determined that the 15th Battalion had taken part in a single action that brought death to 369 partisans, 1,274 suspected persons, and 8,350 Jews, the following exchange took place:

B. And they say it was the 15th Battalion.
s. And they said 15th Battalion was involved.
B. If I got a rifle, I shoot him, that historian. He's a liar.
s. Well, the historian isn't lying. He's got a document.
B. Document, document, who create the document—
    KGB. [The reference is to the Soviet secret police.]
s. Well, the Germans created the document.
B. No, KGB.

When, at the end of the hearing, the discussion turned to the possibility of a court action, Bauzys said:

> At my age. You know I called today my kids, very, very, disappointed. They say that Dad are you a killer? I say no. I killed nobody.[92]

Pure fabrications were a diverse lot. They could be made-up cover stories presented by former collaborators in applications to U.S. immigration officials.[93] In isolated instances they were deceptive claims in a report, such as that of Staatsrat Harald Turner who boasted that Serbia was the only country in which the Jewish *and* the Gypsy problems had been solved, without pointing out that whereas Jewish and Gypsy men had been shot, only Jewish women and children had been gassed.[94] In Denmark the German plenipotentiary, Werner Best, issued an announcement that the Jews had "morally and materially abetted" Danish sabotage. The statement was a typical propagandistic justification for a roundup of the Jews that day. The Danes, as might have been expected, ignored this lame excuse, but the Foreign Office in Berlin actually wanted details. Best had to explain that the assertion was not based on evidence and was intended only to serve the purpose.[95]

More complicated is a false claim to have been an eyewit-

92. Transcript of sworn interview of Jonas Bauzys, June 23, 1992, *United States v. Bauzys*, Civil Action No. TCA 92-40 231 WS. At trial, the judge accepted the defense motion that Bauzys was too ill to be tried.

93. Alan A. Ryan, *Quiet Neighbors* (New York, 1994), pp. 21–24.

94. Turner to Löhr, August 29, 1942, Nuremberg trials document NOKW-1486. The 292 interned Gypsy women and children were released from the Semlin camp; the Jewish women and children at Semlin were gassed in a van. Walter Manoschek, *"Serbien ist judenfrei"* (Munich, 1993), p. 178.

95. Best to Foreign Office, October 18, 1943, Nuremberg trails document NG-5092.

ness. Anyone who misrepresents a tale or a rumor as a first-hand observation has already introduced a falsehood, even if the contents of the story happen to be correct. The falsehood is doubled if they turn out to be wrong.

In the late summer of 1942, the Polish courier Jan Karski was sent by the Polish Government in Exile from London to Warsaw. He saw the Warsaw ghetto very shortly after mass deportations had been conducted there. Following his return he spoke to several people, including President Roosevelt, about his mission. Before the war was over, he described his journey in a book, and much later he repeated the description in public appearances.[96] In several of these accounts, including the wartime book, he mentioned a side-trip in a uniform to Bełżec, where, he said, Estonian guards were stationed, and where a train from Warsaw had arrived. The train, he reported, turned around with its live human cargo, which was then dumped as corpses. In fact there was no contingent of Estonians in the guard force at Bełżec, no trains were sent there from Warsaw, and none ever left there with deportees. Where had Karski been? What had he seen outside the city of Warsaw? The story of trains with deportees moving in and out fit Izbica and several other towns in the Lublin district, where Jews began arriving from Germany in March 1942 and from where Polish Jews were deported to the Bełżec camp after it was ready for gassing.[97] Two biographers of Karski conclude

96. The book was *Story of a Secret State* (Boston, 1944). The meeting with Roosevelt was described by the Polish envoy in Washington, Jan Ciechanowski, *Defeat in Victory* (Garden City, N.Y., 1947), p. 182. A meeting with representatives of Polish Jewry on August 9, 1943, is summarized in American Jewish Archives/World Jewish Congress Collection, Alphabetical files, Poland 205 A-1.

97. Note by Fritz Reuter, Population and Welfare Division, Lublin District, March 17, 1942, and note by Richard Türk, chief of the division, March 20, 1942, Yad Vashem Archives, O 6/11.

that he must have been in Izbica, and that there he could have heard rumors about Bełżec. He had visited the village of Bełżec in 1939.[98]

Much else that Karski recounted was firsthand information. He had brought back messages from Jewish leaders in Warsaw and had taken risks wherever he went. What he had added to his actual experience may have been designed to heighten the attention and awareness of everyone he addressed. In his mind these enhancements might have been justified, and possibly he rejected the thought that they were a form of contamination.

What if an entire story was made up? A purported memoir by an author who called himself Binjamin Wilkomirski was published in Germany and translated into many languages.[99] In this tale he represented himself as a Jewish child survivor. In actuality he was neither a Jew nor a survivor but a Swiss who spent his youth in Switzerland.[100] Given these circumstances, the book is not a source about the Holocaust at all. For researchers concerned with the events of 1933 to 1945, it is a nullity.

98. E. Thomas Wood and Stanislaw M. Jankowski, *Karski* (New York, 1994), pp. 128–130. It would have been difficult for any man in any uniform to enter Bełżec without authorization.

99. Binjamin Wilkomirski, *Bruchstücke* (Frankfurt, 1995), and in English translation, *Fragments* (New York, 1996).

100. See Elena Lappin "The Man with Two Heads," *Granta*, Summer 1999, pp. 7–65.

FIVE

Usability

◻ So far these pages have been devoted to the various elements that were placed in the sources by their creators. Now the focus will be on what may be taken out of the source material by the user. Two separate issues must be considered in that context. One is the sheer challenge faced by a researcher confronting a source. That is a general experience of any historian in any field. The other is a set of specific conditions involving access to Holocaust sources: the when, where, and how of their availability. That is a special factor stemming from a political environment.

The academic problem of a researcher attempting to interpret a source is universal by definition. Holocaust sources, it must be remembered, are sources, and Holocaust research is research. Any enterprise based on sources is empirical, and nothing in this respect distinguishes Holocaust projects from other topics. The methodology is the same and its essentials are clearly recognizable. Stated briefly, they are the following:

1. Any source may have significance.
2. Any difference between sources limits their interchange-ability.
3. Every source is potentially a fragment of a larger config-uration. As maxims these propositions are truisms. They apply to Holocaust research because they cover all historiography.

The first of the three rules deals with a single, unique source, no matter what it is. It may be an order by Adolf Hitler or a list of birthdays of SS officers stationed in Auschwitz. No source, and no part of any source, is unquali-fiedly dispensable. Its importance cannot be fixed by the cir-cumference of its contents, because its relevance is determined by the user alone. To a researcher assessing the mood in the Łódź ghetto, the price paid there for saccharin may be worthy of note. To one who is interested in the daily lives of Byelorussian bystanders, the black market diversions of grain for the clandestine production of alcohol is substantive infor-mation.

Some documentary splinters or even entire files may not seem to be weighty. Adam Czerniaków, for example, who chaired the Jewish Council in Warsaw, noted in his diary re-peated meetings with a German named Avril. In the days be-fore the ghetto was formed, this man inquired about excesses and demanded a report on the activities of the community. Later he and a colleague came to the community offices to in-quire about the Jewish climate of opinion. On another occa-sion he arrived with someone to open the lock of the museum. Thereafter he demanded the draft budget and labor charts. Much later he came to the ghetto to give orders about scenes to be shot for a German propaganda film.[1] Given the mea-sures raining down on Czerniaków almost daily, these subjects

1. Hilberg, Staron, and Kermisz, eds., *Warsaw Diary of Adam Czerni-*

were not exceptional in any way. Franz Avril, however, was a mere SS-sergeant, and in that light the meetings indicate the level to which the highest-ranking Jew of Europe's largest Jewish community had been reduced in the German scheme of things.

By contrast, a forty-eight-year-old Jewish woman, Jenni Cozzi, who was born in northwestern Latvia and was sent to the Riga ghetto, attracted considerable attention among ranking German officials. She was the widow of an Italian officer, and because she held a valid Italian passport, she managed to contact the Italian consulate general in Danzig. The correspondence generated in this case was lengthy. Sturmbann-führer Rolf Günther, who was Eichmann's deputy, wrote to Gesandtschaftsrat Karl Klingenfuss in the German Foreign Office on November 10, 1942, that although Italians (like the late Cozzi) were *artverwandt* (related to Germans in kind), they were not *stammesgleich* (from the same lineage), that the Jewish woman Cozzi could not speak Italian, and that if she were released she would spread atrocity propaganda about the Riga ghetto in Italy. Eichmann himself addressed the Foreign Office, requesting that the Italian embassy be persuaded to cease further intercessions. In like manner, a deputy of the representative of the Foreign Office in Riga wrote to the Foreign Office in Berlin, opposing release. The Foreign Office's expert in Jewish affairs, Eberhard von Thadden, then composed a two-page letter to Eichmann, stating that the Italian emissary would not drop the case. Von Thadden suggested that Cozzi either be freed or that a reasonably acceptable reply

---

akow, pp. 49, 141, 150, 154, 172, 352, 356, 357. Albert Speer, former Reich Minister of War Production, upon reading this diary was struck by the presence of these "minor assistants to those in power, who understood to regiment even the misery." Speer to Benton Arnovitz, editor of Stein and Day, which published the book, November 6, 1978. Courtesy of Mr. Arnovitz.

be given to the Italians for retaining her in the ghetto. A few days later Günther had to inform von Thadden that the High Commissioner of the Fascist party for the occupied eastern territories had intervened for Cozzi. The representative of the Foreign Office in Riga, Adolf Windecker, then wrote to defend the German Security Police view, citing Oberführer Dr. Humbert Achamer-Pifrader, Commander (Befehlshaber) of the Security Police in the Reichskommissariat Ostland. Finally, on September 25, 1943, Eichmann wrote to von Thadden again, referring to the changed political situation in German-Italian relations, and noting that Cozzi would remain in Riga, where the ghetto had in the meantime been transformed into a concentration camp under SS jurisdiction.[2]

If one examines the correspondence file closely, a number of conclusions may be drawn. To start, Sturmbannführer Günther had difficulty in justifying the retention of Cozzi in the Riga ghetto. She could not even speak Italian, he states in one sentence, but she would spread propaganda in Italy, he says in another. Günther's problem is understandable if one keeps in mind how seldom explanations had to be rendered in the first place, and when von Thadden wanted a reason the Italians could accept, it proved to be no simple task. The correspondence as a whole is remarkable for its duration. It is a telling indication of adamancy by Italian officials intent on

---

2. Günther to Klingenfuss, November 10, 1942; Eichmann to Foreign Office, March 5, 1943; Office of the Representative of the Foreign Office in Riga to Foreign Office in Berlin, April 20, 1943; von Thadden to Eichmann, July 2, 1943; Günther to von Thadden, July 6, 1943; Windecker to Foreign Office in Berlin, July 28, 1943; and Eichmann to von Thadden. Correspondence from the archives of the Centre de Documentation Juive Contemporaine, Paris, in Marisa, Giuliana, and Gabriella Cardosi, *Sul confine* (Turin, 1998), pp. 130–136. The authors are sisters whose own mother was deported from German-occupied Italy after all attempts by their Christian father to save her had failed. See *ibid.*, pp. 9–75.

protecting Cozzi and by the Germans to keep her in their stranglehold. Following the Italian surrender to the Allies in September 1943, Eichmann no longer saw any need for further exchanges of letters. That Jews married to Italians were now in a worse situation than Jewish partners of Frenchmen or Germans was a clear measure of how low Italy had sunk in German estimation.

The second principle of utilization refers to likeness and distinctions. Basically, no two sources are exactly alike, which is to say that they are not identical in their entirety. One might, for example, compare two descriptions, both by former SS officers at the Nuremberg trials, of how large-scale killing was conducted in the Crimean city of Simferopol at the end of 1941. The two accounts are remarkably similar in several details as well as manner of expression. The first was given by Obersturmführer Heinz Hermann Schubert, who was the adjutant of the commander of Einsatzgruppe D, Otto Ohlendorf. Essentially Schubert's assignment was to make sure that nothing would go wrong. He relates that the victims were loaded on trucks as quickly as possible and driven a few miles to an anti-tank ditch outside the city. Further, he saw to it that all traffic was diverted from the selected site and that no valuables were pocketed by SS and Order Police personnel. It was also his responsibility to ensure that pursuant to the strict orders of Ohlendorf the shooting with submachine guns and rifles was carried out in a military and, to the extent possible, humane manner. Any other mode of killing, he notes, would have resulted in a psychological burden (*seelische Belastung*) too strong to bear by the Einsatzkommando.[3]

The second statement was made by the chief of Ein-

3. Affidavit by Heinz Hermann Schubert, February 24, 1947, Nuremberg trials document NO-3055.

satzkommando 11b, Obersturmbannführer Werner Braune. Here too, vivid recollections are offered to underscore the orderliness of the procedures. Braune notes specifically that the killing site was cordoned off and that the victims were led in small groups to the ditch, where they had to take off only their heavy winter coats "and the like" to be shot quickly from behind. Even stylistically, Braune echoes Schubert. The adjutant had referred to the victims as "the people designated to be shot" (*zur Erschiessung bestimmten Leute*) and "persons designated for death" (*zum Tode bestimmten Personen*). Braune followed with "people to be executed" (*hinzurichtenden Leute*). There is, however, the following additional assertion of fact in Braune's affidavit:

> I still recall precisely one execution that took place a few days before Christmas in Simferopol. The 11th Army had ordered that the execution in Simferopol was to be ended before Christmas. For that reason we obtained from the army trucks, gasoline, and personnel.[4]

It is to be expected, of course, that two or more accounts of the same matter would have much in common. That at some point they would also diverge is just as probable. Less obvious is a distinction between an original document and an exact copy of it made by a recipient. It is not a contradiction in terms to speak of a retyped item as an original copy if it dates from the time of the events in question. Such duplicates often had a very specific purpose. A two-page report, simply styled *Meldung*, in which the Higher SS and Police Leader Hans-Adolf Prützmann tabulated the results of shooting operations in the Volhynian region, is a singular document noting that in the course of anti-partisan operations from August to Novem-

---

4. Affidavit by Werner Braune, July 8, 1947, *ibid.*, NO-4234.

ber 1942, a total of 363,211 Jews were killed.[5] Prützmann's compilation was reproduced on a typewriter with large letters and sent on by Himmler to Hitler.[6] Although the body of the contents was repeated verbatim, the creation of the replica was a separate, deliberate act with a new addressee.

In short, any distinguishable characteristic imports an additional meaning. Therefore any difference of kind, format, style, or content in the sources limits their equivalence.

Finally, one or more items may be combined. Interlinkage is a means of creating a Gestalt in which one source illuminates another. The quality of that constellation is a function of what has been gathered and the way in which the materials have been joined.

The simplest combination is the connection of two very proximate sources, such as a letter and a reply in an exchange between officials of two agencies, or the draft of a document and its final version. Recognizably close may also be records with a specific shared attribute like the indication of a year in which a person was born. From such listings, age ranges could be constructed for ranking officeholders in the Generalgouvernement,[7] the members of a reserve police battalion,[8] and the incumbents of a Jewish council.[9] Contrasting items may be

5. Report by Prützmann, December 26, 1942, National Archives, Record Group 242, T 175, Roll 124.

6. Himmler to Hitler, December 29, 1942, Nuremberg trials document NO-1128.

7. In the Generalgouvernement there was a concentration of major officeholders who were born in the first decade of the century. See the biographical capsules in Werner Präg and Wolfgang Jakobmeyer, eds., *Das Diensttagebuch des deutschen Generalgouverneurs in Polen* (Stuttgart, 1975), pp. 945–955.

8. The membership of Reserve Police Battalion 101 was "predominantly middle aged." Christopher Browning, *Ordinary Men* (New York, 1992), pp. 181–182.

9. In the larger ghettos of Poland and in Jewish communities elsewhere, the leadership was middle aged, but in fifteen towns of the rural Kreishaupt-

juxtaposed as well, for example the passes of Jews in Tarnopol and those printed "Only for Aryans" (*Nur für Arier*) in the same city at the time of deportations.[10]

A more complex linkage is an association of materials about two developments to explain a single outcome. A case in point is the start of deportations from Slovakia. In a memorandum by Martin Luther, who headed a division of the Foreign Office concerned with Jews, the history of that development is centered on a Slovak offer in January 1942 to hand over 20,000 Jews to the Germans. Himmler was receptive to the idea and told the Foreign Office to request "20,000 young, strong Jews."[11] That is all Luther had to say about the origin of the negotiations, and at first glance the picture would appear to be clear enough. Slovakia was a satellite state created in 1939 and allied with Germany during the war. Its Jewish population was about 90,000, and by 1942 the Slovak government had instituted harsh measures against the Jews. The next step would have had to be drastic, and a Slovak initiative to diminish the number of its Jewish inhabitants would not be implausible. There is, however, another prehistory. About a year and a half earlier, the Slovaks still endured unemployment lingering from depression days. Germany, on the other hand, already had a war economy and recruited foreign surplus labor. It obtained a promise of 120,000 laborers from Slovakia,[12] and

mannschaft Lublin-Land (adjacent to the city of Lublin), the median age was thirty-seven. List dated November 28, 1939, in Archiwum Państwowe w Lublinie, Collection Kreishauptmannschaft Lublin-Land, Sygn. 101, Karta 9–10.

10. Both passes may be found in United States Holocaust Memorial Museum Archives, Accession No. 1997 A 0194 (Ternopil Oblast Archives), Fond 181, Opis 1, Folder 73.

11. Memorandum by Luther, August 21, 1942, Nuremberg trials document NG-2586-J.

12. Yehuda Bauer, *Jews for Sale?* (New Haven, 1994), p. 65.

by October 1, 1941, the Slovak workforce in Germany had reached 80,037.[13] At that point the labor market had changed in Slovakia, and in November the Slovak government suggested the substitution of 10,000 to 20,000 Slovak Jews for non-Jewish Slovaks.[14] The Germans, who were still searching for places to accommodate Jewish deportees from the Reich itself, did not react to the Slovak offer, but when the tender was repeated in January, the idea of Slovak deportations was solidified. The first transport, carrying Jewish women, moved out during the night of March 25–26. Its destination was Auschwitz.[15]

A comparable story is that of the deportations from France. The German military commander of the occupied zone, General Otto von Stülpnagel, had the luxury of a quiet period until the summer of 1941, when a French underground dominated by Communists and other leftists reacted to the German assault on the Soviet Union with isolated assassinations of German officers and soldiers. Following an attempt on a Luftwaffe major, von Stülpnagel wrote to the Quartermaster General of the Army on December 5, 1941, proposing several reprisal measures, including the deportation of one thousand Jews.[16] Nothing could be done about transports for the moment, and in February 1942, von Stülpnagel resigned

13. Edward Homze, *Foreign Labor in Nazi Germany* (Princeton, 1967), pp. 57, 65.

14. Ivan Kamenec, "The Deportation of Jewish Citizens from Slovakia in 1942," in Desider Toth, ed., *The Tragedy of Slovak Jews* (Banka Bystrica, 1992), pp. 81–105, on pp. 83–86. Bauer, *Jews for Sale?*, pp. 65–67.

15. Vlasta Kladivova, "The Fate of Jewish Transports from Slovakia," in Toth, *Tragedy*, pp. 154–155. Kamenec, "Deportation," *ibid.*, p. 91. Danuta Czech, *Kalendarium der Ereignisse im Konzentrationslager Auschwitz 1939–1945* (Reinbek bei Hamburg, 1989), p. 190.

16. Von Stülpnagel to Generalquartiermeister (General Eduard Wagner), December 5, 1941, Nuremberg trials document NG-3571.

to be replaced by his cousin, General Heinrich von Stülpnagel. Under the second Stülpnagel, the first train was sent
out on March 27, 1942, one of many that were to follow.[17]

The relatively large number of a thousand Jews in the context of the suggested reprisal measure in December, coupled
with the resignation in February, suggests an image of an Otto
von Stülpnagel who was not only decisive but insistent. He
was in fact both, but an array of other documents introduces a
twist. Otto von Stülpnagel was a man of the old school,
"rigidly conservative," cold-blooded, goal-directed, and ratio-
nal. He knew that in occupied Slavic regions within the Soviet
Union, Yugoslavia, and Poland, hostages were shot in large
numbers whenever losses were inflicted on the Germans by
partisans. There he might have done the same. He was, however, in France, and with the French authorities he had developed a coexistence that depended on French collaboration,
which he was reluctant to jeopardize. At first he reacted to
every German casualty by ordering the shooting of three
Frenchmen. For Hitler that ratio was much too mild. Seeking
a way out, von Stülpnagel proposed the deportation of the
thousand Jews as a substitute for escalating the executions. His
suggestion to deport the Jews was accepted, subject only to
the availability of transportation, but the French hostages
were not to be spared. Von Stülpnagel judged that he had
failed. On January 15, 1942, he wrote to Hitler and Field Marshal Wilhelm Keitel that he could not square the "mass-
shooting" of Frenchmen with his "conscience."[18]

The deportations from Slovakia and France were not simple affairs. In neither country did they culminate from a linear
progression of events. The additional findings show that in

17. Klarsfeld, *Memorial*, pp. 1–16.
18. Ulrich Herbert, *Best* (Bonn, 1996), pp. 298–305.

each place there was a confluence of two separate developments, and it was this kind of merging that prompted the dispatch of the earliest Jewish transports outside of Poland to Auschwitz.

Ultimately the attribution of significance to sources, or a differentiation between them, or the fitting of pieces into a larger structure, is an act of recognition. These insights may be easy or difficult, but they are impossible if the material is not made available. For decades that was a major problem for Holocaust research.

Generally the following practices have governed the custody and management of records:

1. Records are kept in the organization that created them for as long as needed in house.

2. Records of public agencies are turned over to public archives. Private records, including those of social organizations, firms, or individuals, stay in private hands unless turned over to a library or an archives.

3. Records of central government agencies go to national archives. Regional and local agencies deliver their records to regional and local archives.

4. Materials in public archives are closed to private users if there is a secrecy consideration for national security, or if the privacy of an individual is to be protected. Private archives are opened at the discretion of the bodies that run them.

The origination of a document must not be confused with the record collection in which it may be found. If no copy retained by the sender is discovered, the document will only be a part of the records kept by the recipient. Often, private letters to public offices may have survived only in those offices. Reports of Jewish councils in several destroyed ghettos of eastern Europe were preserved only in the records of German supervisors. The railroad document sent out from Berlin for the dispatch, among others, of trains to Auschwitz, could be located only in Minsk, even though no transports were scheduled to leave from that city to the camp,[19] and Himmler's order of 1941, about the proper conduct of shooting, was found only in Riga.[20]

A special complication for the custody of the records arose when Germany collapsed in 1945. Substantial collections of central German agencies were brought to Washington and Moscow. In Berlin the United States government held the personnel files of Nazi party and SS men. War diaries and reports of SS units stored by Nazi Germany in Prague remained in the city under Czech control. Wherever the German military and civilian offices abandoned their files in the course of retreats from Soviet territory as defined by its postwar boundaries, there the materials were kept in more than one hundred archives of Soviet republics, regional oblasts, and local municipalities.

From the United States, personnel records of German military officers were released to the new German government after microfilming to facilitate the reconstitution of an army by postwar Germany. Seized industry documents were shipped back as well. The remaining stocks, housed in the Federal Records Center at Alexandria, Virginia, were returned more slowly, after partial microfilming. These were mainly folders of the wartime German army. The Berlin Document

19. Letter telegram by Generalbetriebsleitung Ost/PW (signed by Karl Jacobi), January 16, 1943, United States Holocaust Memorial Museum Archives, Record Group 53.002 (Belarus Central Archives), Roll 2, Fond 378, Opis 1, Folder 784.

20. Himmler to Higher SS and Police Leaders, December 12, 1941, Latvian State Archives, Fond 83, Opis 1, Folder 80.

Center, with its party personnel files, was not turned over to the German Federal Archives until 1994, after microfilming. The Soviet government, on its part, restituted documents of the old Interior and Finance ministries, as well as other items, to the (Communist) German Democratic Republic *Zentralarchiv* in Potsdam, but the Soviets held on to significant quantities of German records, including a collection of Auschwitz documents.

Special Jewish archives were created for items bearing directly on the Jewish fate. In New York the YIVO Institute obtained records of German agencies in eastern Europe and broken collections of some Jewish councils, such as those of Łódź and France. In Warsaw a Jewish Historical Institute (the Żydowski Instytut Historyczny) was created for such materials, and in Paris the Centre de Documentation Juive Contemporaine became a similar resource institution. A few years after the founding of Israel, the government of that country established Yad Vashem for the ingathering of diverse German documents in Photostats and original Jewish council records, diaries, and testimony.

For all practical purposes, the eastern European archives, with the exception of those of Poland, were not accessible to researchers until shortly before the demise of the Communist system. In the West the opening of records was gradual. Thus the holdings of the Federal Records Center at Alexandria, Virginia, were closed to the public until a partial declassification in the mid-1950s. The Alexandria collection, on 28,000 linear feet of shelf, was technically under United States and British control, and releases could be made only by agreement between the two countries. In principle, individual items were not to be let out, and before any collection was to be made available the two governments had to be certain that nothing involving cold war security interests was revealed. Such sifting, however, was not considered worthwhile by the British partners.[21]

Two postwar developments led to exceptional publications of documents. The first was the advent of criminal trials by the Allies, the governments of former satellite states, and the new German and Austrian authorities themselves. Trials of high-ranking Germans were conducted at Nuremberg by the Allies during the second half of the 1940s. For these proceedings the prosecution relied primarily on documents that had been signed or received by the accused. The assembled records, taken from various collections in the custody of Allied powers, were given accession numbers, so that any two items in numerical succession did not necessarily indicate proximity of content. For the first trial, against the "major war criminals," 7,617 numbers were assigned to prosecution documents and affidavits, and for twelve subsequent proceedings, 31,180. The items for the twelve trials were divided into four series: NG (civilian ministries) with 9,890 numbers; NOKW (military) with 3,572; NI (industry) with 15,679; and NO (Party and SS) with 6,039. Defense items were more numerous, but they included many affidavits containing character references and explanations. In all, the selections for the Nuremberg trials were not encompassing. Some important agencies, formations, and corporations were not represented in the defendants' docks. The regional level was not fully reflected, and local offices received little attention.

Over a much longer time, many more trials were held in Germany and other countries of lower-ranking individuals

21. Raul Hilberg to Major John K. Orr, Office of the Secretary of Defense/Office of Public Information/Security Review Branch, January 4, 1952. Orr to Hilberg, February 1, 1952, and note of telephone conversation between Orr and Hilberg, February 4, 1952. The correspondence and my note are in my possession.

whose involvement was so direct and so extreme that they could be charged with murder.[22] The vista of killers in the field was constructed not only of documents but extensive testimony by perpetrators and local witnesses. Testimony was also gathered and preserved by Soviet and Polish investigation commissions and used in trials as needed. Some indigenous collaborators from eastern Europe who had migrated to Western countries were pursued many years afterward in extradition, denaturalization, deportation, or criminal proceedings in Western courts.

The second impetus for relinquishing the confidentiality of archival material was political pressure, especially from Jewish organizations. Files of the Vatican and the International Red Cross were made public after these two bodies had been accused of indifference to the fate of large numbers of victims. The Vatican published documents about its wartime activities in a multivolume set,[23] and the International Red Cross opened its records to researchers.[24] The banks of Switzerland were attacked for unhelpfulness and obstructions with respect to deposits of Jews who had not survived and whose heirs faced difficulties in claiming the money. Were these banks to have chosen silence, they would have exposed themselves to the additional reproach of concealment. They could not ignore the charges because the World Jewish Congress and its governmental allies, particularly in the United

22. On postwar German trials, see Adalbert Rückerl, *Die Strafverfolgung von NS-Verbrechen 1945–1978* (Heidelberg and Karlsruhe, 1979).

23. Secrétairie d'État de Sa Sainteté, *Actes et documents du Saint Siège relatifs à la seconde guerre mondiale* (Città del Vaticano, 1965–1980), 10 volumes, of which vol. 3 is in two separately bound books.

24. See the use of this material in Jean-Claude Favez, *Un mission impossible? Le CICR, les déportations et les camps de concentration nazis* (Lausanne, 1988).

States, would threaten boycotts and other dire consequences for these business enterprises at a time when they were poised to expand their foreign investments and markets. A massive investigation, financed by Swiss banks, was consequently conducted to uncover accounts and possible claimants. The results were made public in a report in summary form.[25] This kind of research, not confined to Switzerland, was extended to other companies, in Germany and elsewhere.[26]

One may say that all these revelations were gains of knowledge, but at the same time they were a measure of disproportion and incompleteness. The aims of prosecutors, critics, and claimants are basically different from those of academic researchers. For the former, the gathering of evidence serves a practical end that can be expressed in a specific result: convictions, expulsions, or payments. Once that goal is reached, the quest is over. For the academic person, discovery itself is the purpose, and there is no limit to the desire for understanding. The researcher is interested not only in order givers, executioners, or profiteers but also in initiators, advisers, enablers, and spectators. Central government authorities must

25. See Jost auf der Maur, Daniel Ammann, Erik Nolmans, and Markus Schneider, in three lead articles of *Facts* (Switzerland), August 20, 1998, pp. 16–26, and the news report "Wenn 650 Revisoren 4.1 Millionen Konti prüfen," *Neue Zürcher Zeitung*, December 7, 1999, p. 11. The complete findings are in the Independent Committee of Eminent Persons (Paul Volcker, Chairman), *Report on Dormant Accounts of Victims of Nazi Persecution in Swiss Banks* (Berne, 1999). The Volcker report does not have numbers that confirm a preceding settlement for as much as $1,250,000,000. See the stipulations in the Settlement Agreement, January 26, 1999, for claims under *In re Holocaust Victims Assets*, January 26, 1999, Master Docket CV-96-4849 and other suits covered by the agreement. Federal District Court, Eastern District of New York.

26. Barry Meier, "Chroniclers of Collaboration," *New York Times*, February 18, 1999, p. C1. For the nature of pressure on insurance companies, see *The Insurance Forum* (Special Holocaust Issue), September 1998.

be shown with their regional networks, and the industrial or commercial giants must be paired with the small retailers who acquired new customers or with the small construction companies that employed forced labor or built the concentration camps and gas chambers. This extension of the research effort could not be achieved before the cold war came to an end. Only then did the plenary release of records begin. Although some items remained closed, the rule of general secrecy and exceptional disclosure was reversed. Documents were now selected by their holders for continued confidentiality rather than for necessary accessibility. This shift was possible because the bulk of the sources could be deemed "historical."[27]

The opening of the archives presented an opportunity to the United States Holocaust Memorial Museum and Yad Vashem to copy original documents on microfilm. In the rolls, which can contain about a thousand images on 32-millimeter microfilms and nearly two thousand on 16-millimeter films, materials from many locations across Europe could be concentrated in Washington and Jerusalem. The life of a film is also much longer than the brittle wartime paper of the original records, particularly if they have been exposed to the air and handled frequently by archivists and users. On the other hand, microfilming is seldom comprehensive. The United States Holocaust Memorial Museum, for example, obtained copies of finished microfilms, that is to say material that had already been sifted by an agency or institute abroad, such as

27. The Special Archives in Moscow ("Osoby") was in fact restyled the "Center for Preservation of Historical Documentary Collections," and the German materials left in Prague were held in a renamed *Vojensky Historicky Archiv* ("Military Historical Archives"). In Paris an international conference of archivists was devoted to presentations on Holocaust holdings. See Centre de Documentation Juive Contemporaine, *Les archives de la Shoah* (Paris, 1998). See also the center's *Guide europeén des sources d'archives sur la Shoah* (Paris, 1999).

the Polish war crimes commission or the Jewish Historical Institute in Warsaw. The eastern portions of Poland that had become a part of the Soviet Union were visited by museum teams, but as a matter of practical necessity they had to make compromises of their own. If, for example, one examines Roll 1 of four microfilms made in the Ternopil (formerly Tarnopol) Oblast archives, the results look like this: Fond (collection) 181, Opis (subcollection) 1, Folder numbers 2, 3, 8, 10, 38, 53, 71, 72, 73, 91, 98, 108, 109, 110, 111, 112, 143, 169, 170, 172, and 176.[28]

Microfilm copies are black and white, and therefore any other color, as found from time to time on the originals in color-coded handwritten comments or initials, is lost. Some films obliterate copied material in an all-black or all-white mass, and in the case of wartime reports on which the reverse side of a sheet was used for the second page, the text may be illegible. Even in good films, numbers and signatures may be hard to discern.

Whenever folders are transferred from one archives to another, the original archival document numbers are usually changed. Sometimes these changes are made twice or even three times. Thus if a researcher makes use of an item before it reaches its final resting place, a concordance may be needed to find it again. If an item is taken from a microfilm, and that film does not contain a picture of the folder cover, a problem may arise when the original document should be consulted. In addition there may be "contamination," which is defined as any writing by an archival custodian on the cover or the pages, including renumeration of page numbers. Finally, one must not overlook the time it takes to microfilm a collection, as well

28. United States Holocaust Memorial Museum Archives, Accession No. 1997 A 0194 (Ternopil Oblast Archives), Roll 1.

as the additional time needed to construct finding aids for the films.

Researchers do not wait until all the archives are open to them. They begin with whatever is at hand. Already before the end of the war, the nature of Nazi Germany's organization and actions was studied on the basis of laws and other published materials. Some of these studies proved to be foundational, such as Ernst Frankel's *The Dual State* (New York, 1941), which showed how discriminatory court decisions were developed against Jews alongside a traditional system that was maintained for the legal relations of Germans among themselves; or Franz Neumann's *Behemoth* (New York, 1942 and 1944), which set forth how four power structures—the civil service, the military, industry, and the Nazi party—operated in large measure independently of one another; or Raphael Lemkin's *Axis Rule in Occupied Europe* (Washington, D.C., 1944), which revealed the similarities of discriminatory laws of several European countries on Germany's side, and in which Lemkin coined the word "genocide."[29]

The Nuremberg documents as well as the trial testimony of many proceedings formed the principal source base of many postwar works. As early as 1947, Léon Poliakov was able to use approximately 150 prosecution items introduced in the Nuremberg trials, together with a few other documentary sources, to publish the first coherent account of the steps leading to the annihilation of European Jewry.[30] The availability of the Einsatzgruppen reports and ancillary items allowed Helmut Krausnick and Hans-Heinrich Wilhelm to prepare a heavy monograph on the development of mobile killing in the

29. All three of the authors were lawyers. Neumann, whose model of four independent hierarchies is reflected in the classification of the Nuremberg subsequent trial documents, was also a political scientist. Lemkin was a specialist in public international law.

30. Léon Poliakov, *Bréviaire de la haine* (Paris, 1951).

occupied USSR.[31] The testimony of ordinary men in a police battalion enabled Christopher Browning to probe the psyche of these individuals as they faced their victims at close range.[32] With the accessibility of internal German correspondence in the German Federal Archives, Uwe Adam could explore the mechanism of law- and decree-making in the unfolding bureaucratic process, thereby explaining the logical order of accelerating and thickening measures against Jews.[33] With a mix of local decrees and ghetto records, together with published and unpublished diaries and memoirs, Isaiah Trunk drew a picture of the Jewish councils and their administrative machinery in eastern Europe, revealing a common underlying Jewish response pattern in the isolated communities.[34]

The surge of archival material opened to inspection upon the end of the cold war facilitated a new wave of studies. A deeper look into regional scenes emerged, and some of the books dealt with a country or a province.[35] Other investigations were focused on overlooked organizations.[36] Still others, drawing on fuller correspondence files, segmented events into ever smaller slices of time, thereby demarcating phases and transitions more sharply.[37]

31. Krausnick and Wilhelm, *Die Truppe des Weltanschauungskrieges.*
32. Browning, *Ordinary Men.*
33. Uwe Adam, *Judenpolitik im Ditten Reich* (Düsseldorf, 1972).
34. Trunk, *Judenrat.*
35. For example, Michael Marrus and Robert Paxton, *Vichy France and the Jews* (New York, 1981); Walter Manoschek, *"Serbien ist jundenfrei"* (Munich, 1993); and Dieter Pohl, *Nationalsozialistische Judenverfolgung in Ostgalizien* (Munich, 1996).
36. Wolf Gruner, "The German Council of Municipalities (*Deutscher Gemeindetag*) and the Coordination of Anti-Jewish Local Politics in the Nazi State," *Holocaust and Genocide Studies*, vol. 13 (1999), pp. 171–199. The article deals with the nonadmissibility of Jewish merchants to flea markets and with the role of pawnshops in confiscations.
37. Notably the book by Peter Longerich, *Politik der Vernichtung* (Munich, 1998).

In far greater measure than before, the Holocaust can also be placed in a larger framework. The "racial ladder" in the concentration camps could be explored, from Germans, Slavs, and Gypsies, among others, to Jews.[38] Precise links could be established between the euthanasia program and the gas chambers in Bełżec, Sobibór, and Treblinka.[39] Connections could be made between the expulsions of Poles, the "repatriation" of ethnic Germans from eastern Europe, and the concentration of Jews in ghettos.[40] The Holocaust can be related to the war and to events before and after.

In its advanced stages, Holocaust research has given rise to specializations and subspecializations. As the subject is divided into microcomponents, similarities and distinctions may be seen with greater acuity, but there is no finality. Findings are always subject to correction and reformulation. That is in the nature of the empirical enterprise. Since historiography is also an art form, there is inevitably a striving for perfection. Yet the reality of the events is elusive, as it must be, and the unremitting effort continues for the small incremental gains, no matter what their cost, lest all be relinquished and forgotten.

38. Wolfgang Sofsky, *Die Ordnung des Terrors: Das Konzentrationslager* (Frankfurt, 1993).

39. Henry Friedlander, *The Origins of Nazi Genocide: From Euthanasia to the Final Solution* (Chapel Hill, N.C., 1995).

40. Götz Aly, *"Endlösung"* (Frankfurt, 1995).

Index

A NOTE ON THE AUTHOR

Raul Hilberg, the acknowledged master historian of the Holocaust, is professor emeritus of political science at the University of Vermont. His books include *The Destruction of the European Jews* and *Perpetrators Victims Bystanders*, both of which have been published in several languages, and *The Politics of Memory*, a memoir. He has also edited *Documents of Destruction* and (with Stanislaw Staron and Josef Kermisz) *The Warsaw Diary of Adam Czerniakow*. He lives in Burlington, Vermont.